CAMPER VAN COOKING

CAMPER VAN COOKING

From quick fixes to family feasts,
70 recipes, all on the move

Claire Thomson & Matt Williamson

photography by Sam Folan

Hardie Grant

QUADRILLE

For Grace, Ivy and Dot, and for all the other families out there camping whom we've met along the way.

CONTENTS

Cook's Notes

Unless specified otherwise...

Recipes serve 4 people

Use salted or unsalted butter according to what you take with you

Eggs, veg and fruit are medium and fresh

A note on 'cupful'

For the sake of ease, in the recipes '1 cupful', when referring to liquid, is equivalent to about 250ml (9fl oz) water. However, bear in mind that depending on the density of your ingredient – a solid, for example oats or flour or yoghurt; and, how finely chopped or milled it is – a 'cupful' by volume may weigh more or less than the same volume of water. I'm pointing out here that the weight of 1 cupful will vary according to the ingredient. I've given approximate weight equivalents throughout – but this is camper van cooking and here, more so than in other styles of cookery, recipes do tend to be less exacting when it comes to weights and measurements. There are some where it *does* matter, and I take care to point these recipes out, but please enjoy the process and try not to worry. Handfuls, tablespoons and tins all give a similar feel to the recipes in this book.

The Camper Van Cookbook

It is a remarkable feeling to take to the road with ample provisions, shrugging off the day-to-day and household responsibilities, in search of high adventures and a need to reconnect with the world beyond our front door. We are creatures who have roamed for millennia, after all, and deep in our collective make-up is a need to look up at the stars in the sky – or rather, and perhaps a more current phenomenon (certainly for me), a need to switch off from work and spend quality time with my family.

Camping offers a more hand-to-mouth existence and, even if you are staunchly the sort of person who requires running water and electricity to enjoy yourself, living outside, whether for a night, a week or more, allows for a different sort of reality. Freer, certainly; more weathered, definitely, with the rhythm of your day then subject to more base conditions – the need to eat, the need to keep warm and the need to sleep. It is this nascent sense that I so enjoy when it comes to camping, with the heat of the day beginning to fade. Fires are lit for warmth, illumination and also for cooking. People gather, food and heat sources are shared among friends, old and new, and stories are told. There are also those opportunities to camp when you might prefer to go it alone, or at least with fewer people, in search of proper wilderness. When you arrive, as night begins to fall, there is the joy of swinging shut the doors on the camper, setting up the table within, blankets, a deck of cards, some drinks, a meal prepared, the van a cosy beacon in an empty landscape.

I'm quite aware how romantic the notion of all this sounds. And, truth be told, I became a convert to camping only in recent years – since becoming a parent, I suppose. My husband is a Kiwi and, by birthright alone, is a massive fan of camping. Matt delights in telling our three children about his experiences as a child, the entire summer holidays spent under canvas, roaming the outdoors. Hotels can be a pain with a young family, not to mention costly and perhaps even stressful with the exhausting regime of having to temper children's (teenagers', even lively adults') more exuberant and boisterous conduct – behaviour better suited to wide-open spaces.

And so it is that my family and I have found ourselves these past five or so years driving off in a camper van in search of secluded camping spots and, in contrast, the occasional music festival. Beaches, rivers, mountains, forests... having the camper van bolsters my confidence as the more apprehensive, fair-weather camper. Rain, wind or shine, I prefer the sturdy format over canvas, for when we all do (finally) drift off to sleep.

More often than not, our camping party will swell with the odd tent or awning (for hardy friends or plucky children, who have no need for walls) nudging up beside the van, our camp spilling out to accommodate more people for the night, the week, whatever. A flexible space, a movable feast, it is the sense of independence that camping offers that I find compelling. I enjoy the days being punctuated by the making of food and the conviviality of sharing it. I also happen to think that our camping diet should not be inferior to the one we enjoy from the comfort and reliability of the home kitchen. Different absolutely, more portable perhaps, or more likely to be eaten off your lap at the very least, but it is always my aim that it must never be anything less than completely delicious. Some of the recipes in this book make a nod to nostalgia that many find heartening when cooking outdoors. So, yes, marshmallows feature, as do sausages – but I have also tried to ensure, for the most part, that these recipes have a contemporary and intuitive heartbeat that is suited to camping. I hope, too, that they embody the principal idea of how we can achieve imaginative cookery from beyond four solid walls, in the middle of nowhere, in a makeshift kitchen, and even with the rain lashing down.

From my experience, cooking well on a camping trip is primarily about being well organized, so much so that your aim is to become one of those people who merrily declare "*a place for everything and everything in its place*". Perhaps not, but you get the gist. It's very tricky to find a corkscrew in the dark if you haven't put your headtorch in the place where you first think to look for it. I'm including a non-negotiable camper van tool kit and camper van storecupboard in the introduction – both are paramount in allowing you to cook to the best of your ability, conjuring up meals worthy of raucous campsite applause. You might find the manner in which I've listed some of the ingredients in the recipes for this cookbook a bit of an anomaly at first. Let me explain...

While writing the recipes, I decided there were probably very few people who would bother to take a set of scales camping. Therefore, tablespoons, cupfuls, packets and tins are my preferred format for this book's recipes. However, the recipes in chapter one are intended for cooking in advance to take with you, so here I've also given the weights and measurements for each recipe.

As for the rest of the book, I've separated the contents into the different eating scenarios that we encounter in outdoor cookery. I've covered everything from first-night meals (tired-on-arrival sustenance) and one-pot classics (swift, easy-to-assemble) to more ambitious dishes (over flames, open fire, a charcoal grate or gas burner), lunches and picnics (daytime adventures) and sweet provisions (tempting, perhaps even to make new friends).

Above all, this book is a celebration of cooking from a camper van. It's about having the freedom to take off in search of the open road and being able to cook outstanding food when you get there.

Enjoy the ride.

Claire x

Camper van storecupboard
and a note on topping up and fresh produce

The camper van storecupboard is a store of useful ingredients that are appropriate to take camping. What these ingredients bring is a mixture of sustenance, flavour and ease. This is not an exhaustive shopping list – you will need to top up with fresh produce before you leave or buy in situ when you arrive (fresh meat, fish, dairy, eggs, fruit and also bread). Drinks, too. I'll leave those to you, but I would like to note that oat, nut and long-life milks are handy to take camping because they can all be stored at an ambient temperature until opened.

I mention several times in this book my love of a frozen pack of vegetables (peas, spinach and sweetcorn) to take camping, boosting refrigeration until the packet has defrosted. I would also add prawns to this camping hack, but you will need to be more cautious to keep these suitably chilled until use.

This leaves me with a final note on fresh produce. Apart from the first-night meals in Chapter 1, I've steered clear of suggesting fresh herbs to accompany any of these dishes. My feeling is that you are unlikely to take bunches of herbs with you on a camping trip (the straw that breaks a camel's back, did somebody mention that?), except perhaps for the first night. However, by all means embellish any, if not quite all (you'll know the ones) of these recipes if you happen to have fresh herbs to hand. With a lack of fresh herbs in mind, I've used spring onions (scallions) as a seasoning in some of these recipes, treating this hardy and diminutive allium a bit like I would herbs. Lemons and limes – I'm all for using freshly squeezed juice in dressings, marinades and as a seasoning, but it is worth noting that ambient lemon and lime juice, bought in one of these squeezy bottles can come in handy – not to rival fresh citrus, but a useful ingredient for the camping storecupboard nonetheless. And finally, finally, if you're going to take salad leaves camping, a bag of rocket is pretty hardy and you can use it like a herb. But, for the definitive camping salad leaf, I'd recommend little gem lettuces – a sturdy format, they can handle a bit of a tight squash.

Savoury

Bread: baguettes, crusty, focaccia

Canned fish: anchovies, crab, sardines and tuna

Charcuterie, including chorizo and 'nduja (meat products with a good ambient shelf life)

Chickpeas (garbanzos) and beans

Chilli flakes, chilli sauce, harissa and pepper paste

Chopped tomatoes and passata

Coconut milk and cream

Flours: plain and self-raising (self-rising); baking powder and bicarbonate of soda (baking soda)

Good-quality ambient stock

Jarred antipasti vegetables: artichokes, capers, olives, mushrooms and peppers

Oils: olive, sesame and sunflower or vegetable

Packet carbs: pasta, couscous, rice and noodles

Pickled lemons

Pickles: chutney, gherkins, jalapeños and piccalilli

Salt and black pepper (ideally in grinders)

Sauces: brown, fish, hoisin, ketchup, mayonnaise, mustard and soy

Spice/herb store, including sumac and dried oregano

Squeezy lemon and lime juice (in the absence of fresh)

Sweet and drinks

Biscuits (cookies): in particular, digestive biscuits (graham crackers), but also fruit bread, hot cross buns, stroopwaffles and waffles

Canned fruit

Cereals

Chocolate spread/sauce

Custard

Dark (bittersweet) or milk chocolate (bars and/or buttons)

Dulce de leche

Jam

Marmalade

Marshmallows

Nuts

Oats

Peanut butter

Squirty cream

Sugars: caster (superfine), granulated and light and dark brown soft; runny honey and maple syrup

Coffee

Drinking chocolate

Oat and nut milks

Tea

Camper van cooking equipment list

I could get quite techy and nerdy in this equipment list, but I'm not going to, because, to be frank, if you have a camper van and some rudimentary kit on which to cook and serve a meal, then you're doing alright. I am sure there are a good many books on camping that will exhort long must-have lists of gadgets to ensure an unrivalled camping experience, but this just isn't me. I honestly think you can get by with very little – you are camping, after all, in search of the antithesis of your usual domestic goings-on. So, sure, there are some absolute camping bankers and also some luxuries to pack that will make your camp more comfortable and your ability to cook well all the easier, but this list is in no way intimidating. It is straightforward and sensible, which should be reassuring for the hesitant campers among you.

Storing & preparing

Bottle opener and corkscrew

Can opener

Cheese grater

Chopping board, several – at least one for
savoury and one for sweet

Colander

Cool box or plug-in refrigeration unit

Foil

Knives: several, including a bread knife

Large, collapsible water container (plus
refillable water bottles for drinks)

Measuring spoons

Reusable food containers

Scissors

Cooking & serving

Bowls, plates, mugs (I like enamel)

Camping stove: gas or charcoal (we have
both)

Coffee-making kit (I like aeropress or V60),
plus filters

Cutlery (silverware)

Fire equipment: bowl or plate for fires,
grilling or barbecuing, and logs, charcoal,
lighter, matches and eco firelighters

Glasses (good-quality, hard-wearing
reusable plastic)

Kettle

Oven pad or hot holding glove (oven mitt)
for fire and grill work

Pots and pans (I like cast iron)

Tables/chairs

Teapot

Utensils: mixing and measuring spoons,
whisks, ladle, spatula, tongs

Wipe-clean tablecloth

Clearing up

Collapsible plate-drying rack

Dish towels, paper kitchen towel and
paper napkins

Washing-up bowl

Washing-up liquid

Other

Batteries

Lanterns – multi-fuel, gas or LED, also
fairy lights

1

FIRST-NIGHT MEALS
AND BAKES

Crucial to a successful first night away camping is to arrive with the very first meal ready-made, so that all you have to do is warm it up, or simply serve it as it is on a plate, along with some flattering accompaniments. Effortless mealtime preparation (at least, near enough) is crucial here, giving you enough time to set up camp before night-time falls, which can, inevitably, make things just that tiny bit trickier to sort. If you also take some tempting cakes and bakes to slice and hand out as dessert, your skill and proficiency as a camper will never be in doubt. Being able to guarantee an almost home-from-home vibe is the finest camping accolade of all.

With this in mind, these 10 recipes are all perfect to make at home in your own kitchen, with more of your usual ingredients to hand, then pack and take with you camping. Some are even better made the day before, meaning you can really get ahead with your preparations. And one thing to mention here, 24-carat-gold camping advice, is to freeze any of the meals you make that require heating up while camping – the frozen meal will defrost as you travel to your destination, boosting overall refrigeration of any other camping ingredients you may be also be taking. As for the sweet recipes, all have longevity, meaning that as the days roll by, the results will taste better and better, if you can manage to keep them that long.

Chilli beans with tortilla chips, salsa and sour cream

This is the ultimate camping meal. Make it at home with your usual store of spices, then reap the rewards with a quick reheat, giving you enough time to assemble the ingredients to serve – all of which are optional, but worth it. Do away with the chopped salad, if you like, and opt instead for a good-quality, shop-bought salsa. Tortilla chips bring a perfect crunch, and necessary ease when it comes to serving.

2 tbsp sunflower or vegetable oil
1 large onion, finely chopped
2 celery sticks, finely chopped
1 green (bell) pepper, deseeded and
  finely chopped
1 cinnamon stick
2 bay leaves, scrunched a little
3 or 4 garlic cloves, peeled and finely
  sliced
1 tsp hot or sweet smoked paprika
1 tsp cumin seeds, toasted and ground
1 x 400g (14oz) can of chopped
  tomatoes
3 x 400g (14oz) cans of black or kidney

beans, drained and rinsed
chipotle chilli paste or chilli flakes
  (optional), to taste
salt and black pepper

TO SERVE (ALL OPTIONAL)
1 small bunch of coriander (cilantro),
  roughly chopped
sour cream
tortilla chips
4 ripe tomatoes, diced
1 red onion, finely sliced or diced
1 avocado, sliced or diced
hot or chilli sauce

Heat the oil in a heavy-bottomed saucepan over a moderate heat. Add the onion, celery and (bell) pepper with the cinnamon and bay leaves and gently fry for about 10 minutes, until the vegetables are soft and golden. Then, add the garlic, paprika and ground cumin and fry for another couple of minutes.

Add the canned tomatoes, season well with salt and simmer for about 10 minutes, until rich and thick.

Add the beans, mixing thoroughly, then add the chilli paste or flakes to taste. Check the seasoning, adding more salt if necessary and plenty of black pepper. Then, cook over a moderate heat for about 5 minutes for the beans to heat up and the flavours to meld sufficiently. Remove from the heat. If you like, you can mash a portion of the beans with a fork for a creamier texture – not to worry if you prefer not to.

To serve, reheat the beans if necessary, and serve strewn with coriander (cilantro), and with sour cream, tortilla chips and a salad of chopped tomatoes, red onion and avocado (or a jar of ready-made salsa) on the side. Hot sauce for me – always.

Soup of borlotti beans, potato and small pasta

This recipe tastes even better the day after it is made, wallowing in the cooking liquid, imbuing beans, pasta and potatoes with the rosemary, garlic and chilli. I'd say the result is half soup, half stew – you'll want to eat it with a spoon and a great big hunk of crusty bread to mop up, smudging the bread into the potatoes and the beans. Why have just one carbohydrate, when you can have four in one meal? This is hairs-on-your-chest-type eating – a good thing, and perfect for camping.

4 tbsp olive oil, plus more to serve
1 onion, finely chopped
3 celery sticks, finely chopped
1 large rosemary sprig, needles picked and finely chopped
3 garlic cloves, finely chopped
pinch of dried chilli flakes, plus more if needed
1 medium floury potato, peeled and finely chopped

2 x 400g (14oz) cans of borlotti (cranberry) beans, drained and rinsed
200g (7oz) small pasta shapes, such as macaroni, or use broken-up spaghetti
salt and black pepper
grated parmesan, to serve
4 slices of your favourite, robust crusty bread

Heat the oil in a large saucepan over a moderate heat. Add the onion, celery and rosemary and fry for about 10 minutes, until the onion is soft and translucent. Add the chopped garlic, the chilli flakes and a good seasoning of salt and cook for 2 minutes more.

Add the potato and the beans along with 1.2 litres (40fl oz) of cold water. Bring the liquid to the boil, reduce the heat and simmer for 15 minutes, until the potatoes are soft and cooked through.

Next, add the pasta. Increase the heat and bring the liquid back to the boil and cook until the pasta is al dente. You may need to add a splash more water if it gets too dry. Stir often to prevent the pasta, beans and potato from sticking.

Remove from the heat, check the seasoning, adding more salt and chilli flakes if required, and serve each bowl with an extra slick of olive oil and plenty of parmesan, and with slices of bread on the side for dipping.

Beef cooked with coconut, lemongrass and turmeric

A rendang, as this dish is called in Sumatra, uses the method of braising the meat first in the coconut milk, which then ends up almost frying in the oil as the liquid reduces. I've written this recipe in its simplest form to make it suitable to take camping. Serving ideas are vast and exciting, but I'm suggesting here shake-them-out-of-a-packet crisp-fried shallots and crushed peanuts – an easy fix to take with you. Serve alongside some cooked rice or rice noodles. Shop-bought roti bread is also good to drag through the sauce, helping to clean the plates, too.

3 shallots or 1 small red onion, roughly chopped
5 garlic cloves, roughly chopped
2 tbsp grated fresh ginger
1 tsp ground turmeric
2–4 bird's-eye chillies or 1 tbsp chilli flakes, or to taste
3 tbsp sunflower or vegetable oil
2 lemongrass stalks, halved and bruised slightly
6 lime leaves
1 star anise
1 cinnamon stick
800g (1lb 12oz) braising beef, cut into 3cm (1¼in) dice

1 x 400ml (14fl oz) can of full-fat coconut milk
1 tbsp seedless tamarind pulp
½ tsp salt, plus more to taste if needed
1 tsp palm or white sugar, plus more to taste if needed

TO SERVE
½ cupful peanuts (about 80g/2¾oz), crushed
30g (1oz) desiccated coconut (about 6 tbsp), lightly toasted in a dry pan
cooked rice or noodles, or roti (flat bread)
lime wedges

Blend the shallots, garlic, ginger, turmeric and chillies to a smooth paste, adding a splash of water if required.

Heat the oil in a large frying pan. Over a low heat, gently fry the paste for about 5 minutes, until it begins to stick to the bottom of the pan.

Add the lemongrass, lime leaves, star anise and cinnamon stick. Turn up the heat to moderate and add 100ml (3½fl oz) of cold water. Bring the mixture to a simmer and gently cook for 10–15 minutes, until completely dry and sticky, with all the water absorbed.

Add the beef and cook gently for 10 minutes, then add the coconut milk, 100ml (3½fl oz) of water, and the tamarind, salt and sugar. Simmer on a low–moderate heat for 45 minutes–1¼ hours, until you have a dark brown, rich-tasting curry sauce and the beef is tender. Add a spoonful of water here and there throughout the cooking process if the pan gets too dry. Check for seasoning, adding more salt or sugar to taste.

Serve the curry sprinkled with the peanuts and coconut and with cooked rice or noodles, or roti on the side.

Country pork terrine

Terrines often come with a sort of cheffy, restaurant context – it's a shame, really, as they are incredibly easy to make (quality ingredients and patience pay off) and provide a good, portable, hearty meal. Take this rustic terrine with you for the first night's camp and slice it to serve with good mustard or chutney, some pickles, a chunk of cheese and good crusty bread or sturdy crackers.

600g (1lb 5oz) coarsely minced or finely chopped fatty pork
300g (10½oz) rindless unsmoked streaky bacon, ½ finely chopped
50ml (1¾fl oz) brandy, port or wine
¼ tsp ground nutmeg
½ tsp ground allspice
½ tsp black pepper, plus more if needed
1 tbsp chopped sage or thyme leaves
50g (1¾oz) butter or lard, plus more to grease

2 large shallots or 1 onion, finely chopped
3 garlic cloves, finely chopped
1 egg, beaten
1 tsp salt, plus more if needed
3 bay leaves

YOU WILL NEED
1 x 900g (2lb) terrine mould or loaf tin

Put the pork and chopped bacon in a large bowl and add the brandy, the spices and the sage or thyme. Mix well, cover and place in the fridge to marinate for a minimum of 30 minutes, and even overnight.

Melt the butter or lard in a pan over a moderate–low heat, then add the shallots or onion and the garlic and cook for 8–10 minutes, until soft and translucent. Remove from the heat and leave to cool. Then, stir the shallot mixture into the meat mixture along with the egg and salt. Mix well to combine.

Put the remaining bacon in between a couple of pieces of greaseproof paper and use a rolling pin to flatten it out, rolling it assertively, until just about doubled in size.

Grease the mould with a little butter or lard, then line it with the pieces of bacon (try not to leave any spaces so that the terrine is completely covered in the bacon when you cook it) and place it in the fridge.

Take a little portion of the terrine mixture and fry it off with a spot of oil in a pan over a moderate heat, then taste to check the seasoning. Add more salt and pepper to adjust if necessary. The terrine will need to be well seasoned because it will be served cold.

Preheat the oven to 180°C/160°C fan/350°F/Gas 4 and boil some water in a pan or kettle.

Place the terrine mixture in the bacon-lined mould, pressing it down firmly and smoothing over the top, fold over any overhanging bacon, neatly, to seal the top of the terrine. Lay the bay leaves in a row on top.

Put the terrine on a dish towel in a deep roasting tin and pour in boiling water to come halfway up the sides of the mould. (The dish towel will prevent the mould from slipping.) Bake the terrine for about 1–1½ hours, until it begins to shrink away from the sides of the mould. If you have a meat thermometer, the internal temperature should read 70°C/160°F. Alternatively, a skewer inserted into the centre of the terrine should come out piping hot – too hot, almost, if tested on the inside of your lip, for your lip to bear.

Remove the cooked terrine from the oven and leave it in the mould for at least 30 minutes, until cold. Then, wrap it tightly and refrigerate. Maturing the terrine for a day or so allows for the flavours to fully develop, and it will keep well for up to 5 days in the fridge.

PICTURED OVERLEAF

Lamb and date tagine

Making a good tagine is a masterclass in balancing flavour. Meat, spice and fruit – all three must be in harmony. Use beef and prunes in similar amounts if you prefer these to lamb and dates. Either way, serve with couscous – pour over boiling water with a pinch of salt, soak, then fluff with a fork when soft and tender – the easiest of accompaniments for this fragrant, gently spiced stew.

50g (1¾oz) butter or 50ml (1¾fl oz) olive oil
600g (1lb 5oz) lamb (shoulder is best), cut into 3cm (1¼in) dice
1 tsp salt, plus more if needed
1 x 400g (14oz) can of chopped tomatoes
2 onions, finely chopped
3 garlic cloves, finely chopped
½ tsp chilli flakes, or more to taste
2 tsp cumin seeds, toasted and ground
2 tsp coriander seeds, toasted and ground

1 tsp ground turmeric
1½ tsp ground ginger
1 cinnamon stick
1 small orange or 1 lemon, 2 small strips of zest removed and reserved
2 tbsp runny honey
16 dates, pitted, or 12 dried apricots
black pepper

TO SERVE
50g (1¾oz) whole almonds, chopped
couscous, cooked as per the instructions on the packet

Melt half the butter in a small saucepan, then transfer it (or half the olive oil) to a large bowl and mix it together with the lamb, salt, tomatoes, onions, garlic and all of the spices. Cover and leave refrigerated for at least a couple of hours – overnight is ideal.

To cook, put the marinated meat in a large heavy-bottomed saucepan. Add the remaining butter or oil and cook the meat over a moderate–low heat, uncovered, for 20 minutes, stirring from time to time.

Meanwhile, halve the orange or lemon, squeezing and reserving the juice from one half and reserving the remaining half to cut into wedges later, to serve.

After 20 minutes, add 400ml (14fl oz) of water to the saucepan, along with the honey, orange or lemon zest and the juice, and the dates or apricots. Stir to combine and reduce the heat to low, then cover and simmer very gently for about 1–1½ hours, or until the meat is melting and tender. Check the tagine from time to time to ensure it doesn't catch, adding a splash more water to the pan if you think it needs it.

Check the seasoning, adjusting with salt and pepper to taste – you want a heady mix of savoury, sweet and spice, with the lamb and its sauce in perfect balance. Refrigerate, or freeze, to take camping.

To serve, heat the tagine over a moderate heat until piping hot and serve topped with the almonds with couscous and orange or lemon wedges on the side.

Giant sausage roll and coleslaw

Make these sausage rolls at home, then bake them just before you leave – blistered, buttery cylinders of pastry, all dense and juicy with pork and fresh sage and thyme. These are mighty sausage rolls and are perfect alongside some coleslaw, which you can also make before you set off.

FOR THE SAUSAGE ROLL
800g (1lb 12oz) pork mince (ground pork)
100g (3½oz) fresh breadcrumbs
100ml (3½fl oz) cold chicken stock, or water
1 tbsp finely chopped sage or thyme leaves (or a combination of both)
big pinch cayenne pepper or chilli powder (optional, if you like a bit of a kick)
1 tsp salt, plus more if needed
400g (14oz) puff pastry

1 egg, lightly beaten
salt and black pepper

FOR THE COLESLAW
50g (1¾oz) crème fraîche or sour cream
50g (1¾oz) mayonnaise
1 tbsp Dijon mustard
¼–½ small white cabbage, finely shredded
1 or 2 carrots, peeled and coarsely grated
½ white onion, very finely sliced
juice of ½ lemon, or 1 tbsp cider or white wine vinegar

First, make the sausage roll. Preheat the oven to 180°C/160°C fan/350°F/Gas 4. Line a baking tray with greaseproof paper.

Put the meat, breadcrumbs, stock, herbs, spice and salt in a large bowl and mix well until combined. Break off a little piece and fry it off in a hot frying pan to check the seasoning. Adjust the seasoning in the mixture, if needed.

Roll out the pastry to a rectangle measuring about 40 x 25cm (17¾ x 10in) and brush it with beaten egg.

Shape the meat filling into a long sausage shape along the length of the pastry, then fold over the pastry and crimp the join together with a fork. Cut into 4 equal pieces and brush the tops with egg. Transfer the rolls to the lined baking tray and bake for 40–50 minutes, until golden brown and cooked through. (If you have a meat thermometer the internal temperature should read 70°C/160°F, or a skewer inserted into the centre should come out piping hot.)

While the sausage rolls are baking, make the coleslaw. Mix together the crème fraîche or sour cream, mayonnaise and mustard, seasoning well with salt and pepper to taste. Assemble all the remaining ingredients in a mixing bowl, then add the mayonnaise mixture and mix well to combine. Transfer to an airtight container and store in the fridge until you're ready to go.

When the sausage rolls are cooked, remove them from the oven and leave them to cool for 10 minutes on the tray, then transfer to a wire rack to cool completely.

Banoffee bread

Banana bread is textbook camping food. It lasts well – in fact, I'd go so far as to say it eats better the day after it is made, turning more fudgy, denser and more intensely banana-y. Toasted, day-old banana bread makes for a heroic breakfast, good for all the family, and also goes particularly well with a cup of coffee. I've upped the ante here for this version, adding chopped caramel, dark chocolate and crunchy biscuits, so yes, you could call this banoffee bread. Why not?

75g (2½oz) butter, melted, or 75ml (2½fl oz) sunflower or vegetable oil

4 very ripe bananas, mashed, plus 1 extra banana, sliced, to decorate

1 egg, beaten

125g (4½oz) light brown soft sugar

40g (1½oz) 70% dark (bittersweet) chocolate, chopped small

1 packet of chocolate-coated soft caramel sweets (candies) (about 7, or 40g/1½oz), chopped small

pinch of salt

180g (6¼oz) plain (all-purpose) flour

1 tsp bicarbonate of (baking) soda

4 digestive biscuits (graham crackers), roughly crushed

Preheat the oven to 160°C/140°C fan/315°F/Gas 2–3. Grease and line a 10 x 20cm (4 x 8in) loaf tin.

If you're using butter, melt it in a small pan over a low heat, or use a microwave. Let it cool slightly but don't let it solidify.

In a mixing bowl combine the melted butter (or the oil), mashed banana, egg, sugar, chocolate, soft chocolate caramels and salt. Add the flour and bicarbonate of soda, mixing briefly to combine. Pour the mixture into the prepared tin and evenly sprinkle over the crushed biscuits.

Bake for 45–50 minutes – checking towards the end of the cooking time and covering with a square of loose foil if the biscuits begin to get too dark, until a skewer inserted into the centre of the cake comes out clean. Remove from the oven and cool in the tin on a wire rack for at least 10 minutes before turning out and leaving to cool completely.

Ginger treacle traybake

Treacle, ground ginger, cardamon, allspice and cinnamon... a cake but not really. You want this traybake to be almost tar-black, a richly spiced and indescribably squishy slab of not-quite cake, soft enough to taint your teeth with a dark, gingery and treacle stain. Gets better and better this one – 2 days, 3 days or more for prime condition.

MAKES 12 SQUARES

225g (8oz) butter
225g (8oz) dark brown soft sugar
225g (8oz) black treacle (molasses)
2 eggs, beaten
175g (6oz) plain (all-purpose) flour
150g (5½oz) wholemeal (wholewheat) flour (or spelt or rye flour)

50g (2¾oz) rolled oats
pinch of salt
2 tsp ground ginger
pinch of ground cardamom
1 tsp ground allspice
1 tbsp ground cinnamon
1¼ cupfuls whole milk (about 300ml/10½fl oz)
2 tsp bicarbonate of (baking) soda

Preheat the oven to 150°C/130°C fan/300°F/Gas 2. Line a 20 x 30cm (8 x 12in) loose-bottomed traybake tin with greaseproof paper.

In a pan over a moderate heat, mix the butter, sugar and treacle (molasses), stirring until melted and combined. Remove from the heat and leave to cool a little until just warm.

Add the eggs to the mixture in the pan, stirring well to combine. Then, add the flours, oats, salt and spices and stir to form a batter. Add the milk, stirring well to combine. Finally, sprinkle the bicarbonate of (baking) soda over the top of the mixture, then stir briefly to combine.

Pour the mixture into the prepared tin and bake for 50 minutes–1 hour, until a skewer inserted into the centre of the cake comes out clean. Remove from the oven and leave to cool in the tin before cutting into squares.

Oat and chamomile cookies

I'm a huge fan of chamomile in baking. Choose the contents of good-quality chamomile teabags or use loose tea, and simply add to all manner of cakes, biscuits and batters. In these cookies, the chamomile flavour pairs brilliantly with the oats and butter – it's a good cookie to serve with a cup of tea or hot chocolate before bedtime, perhaps. These will last well for up to 3 days if stored in an airtight container.

MAKES ABOUT 20 COOKIES

125g (4½oz) plain (all-purpose) flour
½ tsp bicarbonate of (baking) soda
pinch of salt
3 chamomile teabags
110g (3¾oz) butter, softened

150g (5½oz) golden caster (superfine) sugar, or use regular white caster sugar
1 egg, beaten
150g (5½oz) rolled oats

In a large mixing bowl, mix together the flour, bicarbonate of (baking) soda, salt and the contents of the teabags, then put to one side.

Put the butter and sugar in a mixing bowl or the bowl of a stand mixer fitted with the paddle and beat for 2–3 minutes, until creamy. Add the egg and beat well to combine. Add the flour mixture and briefly beat to combine. Finally, add the oats and beat briefly to incorporate.

Put the prepared cookie dough in a tub or covered bowl and refrigerate for at least 30 minutes to firm up.

Preheat the oven to 180°C/160°C fan/350°F/Gas 4. Line a baking tray with greaseproof paper.

Remove the cookie dough from the fridge. Break off enough to roll a ping-pong-sized sized piece of dough in your hands, then flatten the ball slightly and place it on the lined tray. Repeat for the remaining dough, leaving a bit of space between each cookie to allow them to spread during baking (you should get about 20 cookies – make them in batches, if necessary; or refrigerate and use the dough when you need it).

Bake for about 10 minutes, until crisp at the edges but still ever-so slightly soft in the middle. Remove from the oven and transfer each batch to a wire rack to cool while you bake the next.

Peanut butter brownies

Peanut butter is meant for brownies, and salted peanuts scatter extra magic over this rich and decadent slab of chocolate, which is bound together with such a scant amount of flour, eggs, sugar and butter, then baked with such a lean cooking time, you'll wonder how on earth it will hold together when it comes out of the tin. It will, it just needs to cool completely first. There are few things more disappointing in life than an overcooked brownie.

MAKES 16

100g (3½oz) butter
200g (7oz) light brown soft sugar
300g (10½oz) good-quality 70% dark
  (bittersweet) chocolate, broken into
  small pieces

4 eggs, beaten
70g (2½oz) plain (all-purpose) flour
  (or rye flour)
100g (3½oz) smooth peanut butter
30g (1oz) salted peanuts

Preheat the oven to 160°C/140°C/315°F/Gas 2–3 and line a 20 x 30cm (8 x 12in) baking tin with greaseproof paper.

In a large pan over a moderate heat, mix the butter and sugar, stirring until melted and combined. Remove from the heat, then add the chocolate, mixing well until melted and smooth. Mix in the beaten eggs, followed by the flour, and beat until very smooth and glossy. Pour the brownie batter into the prepared tin.

Using a teaspoon, add spoonfuls of peanut butter to the top of the brownie mixture, swirling the peanut butter ever-so slightly into the brownie batter. Then, sprinkle over the peanuts evenly.

Bake the brownie for 18–20 minutes – it should still be quite wobbly in the centre. Remove from the oven and leave to cool completely in the tin before cutting into squares.

2

COOKING ON ONE HOB

These recipes are all one-pan, one-hob, one-dish wonders. They are dishes to drum up with little more than a knife, chopping board and single pan or pot. The allure of cooking over an open fire when camping is real, but to be frank, there are absolutely times when all you want to do is flick a switch and for the food you make to be instant, or at the very least, take minutes to make. And, no, I don't mean pot noodles or baked beans, both of which are terrific – but this is a cookbook for camping, after all, and while I'm hopeful that it is as practical as it is approachable, I'm aiming for it to be, at the very least, just a tiny bit ambitious.

This chapter is made up of 14 recipes all made with storecupboard ingredients. Some are supported by fresh produce, perhaps bought on location (locally bought fresh fish and meat; vegetables, too). These are recipes to learn by rote. All will cook perfectly well back home in your kitchen, but they are in this section because, though they are relatively undemanding to make, they deliver on flavour and have a strong sense of right time, right place, in terms of camping. These are meals to sit down and share together, whatever the weather.

Egg-fried rice with prawns, ginger and peanuts

A one-pot favourite although, granted, unless you have any cold leftover rice
to hand, you will have to cook the rice first. This is easy enough, though. Prawns
(shrimp) are a useful ingredient to take camping, as they are readily bought as
a frozen food that can defrost en route to wherever you are going. Please buy
prawns from a sustainable source with good fishery practice.

4 large eggs, lightly beaten
2 tbsp light or dark soy sauce, plus
    more to taste
1 tbsp fish sauce, plus more to taste
6 tbsp sunflower or vegetable oil
2 tbsp grated fresh ginger
3 carrots, coarsely grated
1 bunch of spring onions (scallions),
    green and white parts separated,
    thinly sliced
good pinch of salt

4 cupfuls cooked long-grain white rice
    (about 750g/1lb 10oz)
1 cupful frozen prawns (shrimp),
    defrosted and peeled (about
    250g/9oz)
1 small white 'loose' cabbage (such as
    hispi), shredded
big handful of peanuts, roughly
    chopped, to serve
chilli sauce, to serve

Beat the eggs together with the soy and fish sauce and set aside.

Heat 2 tablespoons of the oil in a wok or a large non-stick frying pan over high
flame. Give the oil a minute to heat up, then add the ginger. Fry the ginger for about
30 seconds, until fragrant, then add the carrots, the spring onion (scallion) whites
and salt and stir-fry for 1–2 minutes, until the spring onion is wilted and lightly
coloured in places. With a slotted spoon, remove to a plate and wipe out the wok
with some dry kitchen towel.

Put the wok back on the high heat and add 2 more tablespoons of oil. Once the oil
is very hot, add the prawns (shrimp) and fry for 2–3 minutes, until the prawns are
cooked through (the flesh should be opaque and hot to touch in the centre of the
prawn). Put the cooked prawns on the plate along with the gingery cooked carrot.

Add the remaining oil to the wok. Once the oil is very hot and just beginning
smoke, add the cooked rice. Fry the rice, ensuring all the grains get coated in the
hot oil.

Add the beaten egg mixture and continue to fry until all the egg is absorbed by
the rice (2–3 minutes). Stir vigorously and keep frying for about 3 minutes, or until
some of the eggy rice begins to caramelize and toast in the pan.

Return the carrots and prawns to the pan. Toss the rice, prawns and cabbage
together until everything is heated through. Check the seasoning, adding more soy
and fish sauce if you like. Serve immediately with the peanuts and spring onion
greens scattered on top, and with chilli sauce to taste.

Mussels cooked with coconut, turmeric and lime

Mussels are one of the most sustainable seafood to eat in the UK. Grown on ropes, they are easy to farm and enable producers to easily replenish stocks. Mussels are also pretty cheap to buy, and cook beautifully in dishes that require a flavoursome soup or broth. Bought live, they have a pretty good fridge life if stored under a clean, damp cloth, and shouldn't smell in any way fishy, which makes them a great seafood ingredient to take camping. Simply tap any open shells on a hard surface and make sure they close to ensure they are still alive, and pull off any barnacles or beards – a fun and easy bit of kitchen prep. Soak the rice noodles in some boiling water, and everything else is pretty much then minutes from being ready.

2 tbsp sunflower or vegetable oil
1 bunch of spring onions (scallions), trimmed and finely sliced
3 garlic cloves, finely sliced
1 red or green chilli, finely sliced (deseeded if you want less heat; or use chilli flakes, to taste)
1 stick of lemongrass, trimmed and roughly chopped
1 tsp ground turmeric

1 tablespoon fish sauce, plus more to taste
1 x 400ml (14fl oz) can of full-fat coconut milk
1kg (2lb 4oz) mussels, debearded and well washed (discard any open mussels that don't close when tapped)
4 portions of rice noodles, soaked as per the packet instructions
1 or 2 limes (depending on juiciness)

Heat the oil in a large saucepan over a moderate heat, then add the spring onions (scallions) and garlic and cook for 2 minutes, or until softened. Add the chilli, lemongrass and turmeric, then add the fish sauce and coconut milk and bring to the boil.

Add the mussels to the pan and keep the heat high. Put a lid on the pan. Cook for 3–4 minutes, shaking vigorously from time to time, until the mussels are cooked and all the shells have opened up (discard any that remain closed). Meanwhile, put the cooked noodles into bowls. Remove the mussels from the heat and squeeze over the lime juice, stirring the pan to combine. Serve immediately on top of the noodles.

Tomato and fennel fish stew
with garlic and oregano bread

Look out for firm, white, locally caught fish at the fishmongers or fish counter, and, if you're cooking this while camping, it's my guess you must be fairly near the sea, so do ask which fish is best and eats well when cooked in a stew such as this one. Serve this with oregano garlic bread, which you can wrap in foil and toast in the fire if you're having one, or wrap and warm it through in a dry pan over a moderate–low heat.

3 tbsp good olive oil, plus more to serve
1 small onion, finely chopped or sliced
3 celery stalks, finely chopped or sliced
3 garlic cloves, finely sliced
pinch of dried chilli flakes (optional), plus more to taste
big pinch of salt, plus more to taste
2 tsp fennel seeds, lightly crushed
1 tsp dried oregano
½ can of chopped tomatoes (200g/7oz) or about 1 cupful chopped fresh tomato
700ml (24fl oz) fish or vegetable stock, or water

700g (1lb 9oz) firm white fish, cut into bite-size pieces
juice and finely grated zest of 1 lemon
black pepper

FOR THE GARLIC AND OREGANO BREAD
3 garlic cloves, crushed to a paste
2 tsp dried oregano
100g (3½oz) butter, softened (about 7 tbsp)
1 large baguette, slashed at 3cm (1¼in) intervals

Heat the olive oil in a wide, shallow pan over a moderate heat. Add the onion, celery and garlic, and the chilli flakes (if using). Season well with the big pinch of salt and some black pepper and cook for 10 minutes, until soft and fragrant.

While that's cooking, prepare the garlic bread. Mash the crushed garlic and the oregano into the butter and season with salt and pepper. Use the mixture to butter the slashed bread. Wrap it in foil and place it on a heat source (in the embers of your campfire or in a dry pan) to allow it to warm through and melt the butter.

Add the fennel seeds, oregano and chopped tomatoes to the onion and celery in the pan and continue to cook for another couple of minutes, until rich and thick.

Add the stock or water and bring to the boil. Turn the heat down to a simmer and add the fish, then cover with a lid and simmer until the fish is opaque and just cooked through – 5–7 minutes depending on the size and thickness of the fish. Add the lemon zest and check the seasoning, adjusting with lemon juice and more salt, pepper and chilli flakes accordingly.

To serve, ladle the stew into bowls with plenty of the sauce and serve with the garlic bread alongside.

Fried cheese toasties with potato, bacon and pickled jalapeños

Never one to stint on double carbohydrates, I feel that if you are going to make a cheese toastie into a meal, what you need is some proper heft to the slices of pan-toasted bread. Boil the potatoes and, while you're at it, cook extra and keep them cool for later use (see page 158 for a potato salad that would suit). Then, slice as many cooked potatoes as you see fit to sandwich between the slices of bread filled with cheese, bacon and jalapeño. And, yes, you must first fry the bacon in the pan, turning it to crisp strips and leaving the fat behind to use to fry the assembled sandwich. Have a napkin (several, even) when ready to eat.

3 medium waxy potatoes, peeled and halved

3 heaped tbsp butter, softened, plus more if needed

8 slices of good white bread (sourdough is ideal)

8 slices of streaky bacon

2½ cupfuls grated Cheddar (about 250g/9oz)

pickled jalapeño chillies, drained, to taste

Boil the potatoes in plenty of well-salted water for about 15 minutes, until tender. Remove from the heat, drain, cool, then cut into slices about 1cm (½in) thick.

Butter one side of each bread slice using about two-thirds of the butter altogether.

Melt the remaining butter in a large frying pan over a moderate heat and add the bacon. Cook for about 2 minutes on each side, until crisp and brown. Remove the bacon from the pan, leaving the fat behind.

Assemble the sandwiches with the buttered side of the bread on the outside: distribute the potatoes, cheese and bacon evenly, and add the drained jalapeño chillies according to how spicy you like your food.

With the fat in the pan and the pan over a moderate heat, fry the sandwiches in batches, pressing them down in the pan to sear and for the bread to bronze and crisp – about 2 minutes each side, until the bread has taken on a good colour and the cheese has sufficiently melted. (I like to use something heavy, like a saucepan filled with water to exert pressure on the sandwich as it cooks.) Add a touch more butter to the pan, if necessary, between batches. Serve immediately.

Rice with peas and parmesan

Much less heartache than risotto, this one. There's no stirring of the rice required – simply rice and peas simmered in one pot with little more than some onion and chicken or vegetable stock for company, plus plenty of parmesan to serve. Buy a good-quality stock cube, boil the kettle and have the hot stock ready to go. This is a Venetian dish of some repute and some would call it heresy to use frozen peas in lieu of spring's first crop, but we are camping, and swerving some culinary pretentions will make for an easier life on the road. A bag of frozen peas will also act as an extra refrigeration boost as they defrost, ready for use.

50g (1¾oz) butter or 50ml (1¾fl oz) olive oil (about 4 tbsp)
1 onion, finely chopped
1½ cupfuls risotto rice (about 330g/12oz)
4 cupfuls hot chicken or vegetable stock (about 1 litre/35fl oz)

3 cupfuls frozen peas, defrosted (about 400g/14oz)
4 tbsp finely grated parmesan (about 50g/1¾oz)
salt and black pepper

Melt the butter or heat the oil in a saucepan over a moderate heat, add the onion and cook for about 10 minutes, until soft and translucent.

Add the rice and the hot stock to the pan. Increase the heat and bring the liquid to the boil, then season well with salt and lots of black pepper. Turn down the heat to moderate and simmer for 13–15 minutes, add the peas and cook for 5 minutes more, until the rice is cooked but still with a slight bite.

Remove from the heat and stir though half the parmesan. Check the seasoning, adding more salt and pepper as necessary. Serve in bowls topped with the remaining parmesan.

Spinach and paneer curry

Paneer is a fresh Indian cheese. It is prepacked in sealed format and has a great shelf life, making it an excellent ingredient to take camping. It's especially delicious cooked in a curry, alongside another trusted ingredient – frozen spinach. I might have mentioned my love for a frozen bag of vegetables acting as an impromptu ice pack en route to any camping destination...

3 tbsp sunflower or vegetable oil, or ideally ghee
1 onion, finely chopped
1 tsp cumin seeds
4 garlic cloves, finely chopped
1–2 green chillies, finely chopped (deseeded if you want less heat)
2 tbsp grated fresh ginger
1 tbsp garam masala, plus more to serve
1 tsp ground turmeric

500g/1lb 2oz paneer (about 2 packs), chopped into bite-size pieces
250g (9oz) frozen spinach, defrosted and drained
about 6 tbsp full-fat natural yogurt
salt and black pepper
cooked rice, or warmed naan or roti bread, to serve
Indian pickles, to serve

Heat the oil or ghee in a saucepan over a moderate heat, add the onion and the cumin seeds and cook for about 10 minutes, until the onion is soft and translucent. Add the garlic, chillies and ginger and cook for 2 minutes, then add the ground spices, stir to combine and heat through for 30 seconds or so, until fragrant.

Add the paneer and stir well, then add the spinach and add a good splash of water (about 100ml/3½fl oz, just under half a cupful) and cook for about 5 minutes, until the spinach is soft and silky and piping hot.

Remove the pan from the heat, stir through the yogurt and check the seasoning, adjusting with more salt and black pepper as necessary. I like to add a big pinch of extra garam masala to each serving, with the rice or bread, and pickles alongside.

Rice noodles with coconut, tomato and cashew nuts

One-pot noodles. Cook the rice noodles according to the packet instructions, then drain them and assemble the remaining ingredients in the pan before adding the noodles back. The tomatoes and the coconut cook together, mottling their juices, almost splitting as a sauce. With lots of lime, lots of fish sauce and as much fresh chilli as you can bear, this is gutsy cooking, and it could not be any simpler – a boon for cooking on one ring.

2 tbsp sunflower or vegetable oil
4 garlic cloves, finely chopped
2 tbsp finely grated fresh ginger
1 tsp chilli flakes, or more to taste
2 lemongrass stalks, halved and lightly crushed
1 x 400g (14oz) can of chopped tomatoes
1 x 400g (14oz) can of full-fat coconut milk

2 tbsp fish sauce
4 portions of rice noodles, cooked according to the packet instructions
1–2 limes (depending on juiciness), to taste
about 4 heaped tbsp roasted cashews, to serve
2 green chillies, thinly sliced lengthways (optional; deseeded if you like less heat), to serve

Heat the oil in a pan over a moderate heat. Add the garlic, ginger, chilli flakes and lemongrass and cook for 30 seconds, until fragrant. Add the tomatoes and cook for 5 minutes, until rich and thickened, then add the coconut milk, fish sauce and 200ml (7fl oz; ½ the tomato can) of water and cook for 5 minutes, until piping hot.

Add the noodles to the pan and squeeze over the juice of the limes to taste. Then, top with the cashews and green chilli (if using) to serve.

Mushroom chimichanga with black beans, smoked paprika and cheese

A chimichanga should be deep-fried, but frying the assembled tortilla in a good depth of cooking oil – enough to seal the wrap, ensuring the cheese doesn't leak as it melts – works perfectly well in a camping scenario. I like to serve these doused liberally with hot sauce, then dunked in sour cream with a chopped salad of tomatoes, red onion and avocado, dressed with lime juice.

2 tbsp sunflower or vegetable oil, plus more for the chimichanga
1 large onion, finely chopped
2–3 garlic cloves, finely sliced
1 tsp hot or sweet smoked paprika
1 tsp ground cumin
6 large mushrooms, or 12 small ones, thickly sliced
2 x 400g (14oz) cans of mixed beans, drained
chipotle chilli paste or dried chilli flakes (optional), to taste
salt

TO ASSEMBLE AND SERVE
4 large tortilla wraps
4 handfuls grated cheese, such as Cheddar; or crumbled feta
hot sauce, to serve
sour cream, to serve

FOR THE SALAD
1 ripe avocado, diced
2 ripe tomatoes, diced
1 red onion, sliced or diced
juice of 1 lime

Heat the oil in a good-size frying pan over a moderate heat. Add the onion and fry for about 10 minutes, until soft and golden, then add the garlic, paprika and cumin and fry for another couple of minutes. Add the mushrooms and continue to cook for 8–10 minutes, until the mushroom liquid has all cooked away.

Add the drained beans, mixing thoroughly, then give the beans a good mash in the pan with a fork or the back of a wooden spoon. Add the chipotle paste or chilli flakes, if using, and season with salt, then cook over a moderate heat for about 5 minutes, until the beans have heated through and the flavours melded. Transfer to a plate to free up the frying pan. Wipe out the pan.

Meanwhile, assemble the salad, combining the avocado, tomatoes and onion in a bowl, dressing with the lime juice and seasoning with salt to taste.

Lay 1 tortilla wrap flat on a clean surface and smother one half of the wrap with the mashed bean and mushroom mixture. Cover the bean mixture with grated cheese and fold the wrap, pressing the edges together to seal tight. Repeat for all the wraps and filling ingredients.

Cover the base of the pan with a good coating of oil and place it over a moderate heat. In batches, gently fry the wraps for 2–3 minutes on each side, until the surface is crisp and golden in places and the cheese within has melted. Remove from the heat and serve with chilli sauce, sour cream and salad on the side.

Baked rice with chorizo and peas

Paella rice, or any short-grain rice (risotto or pudding, for example), studded with onions, pepper and chorizo, and some frozen peas, too, for good measure, then lidded and cooked until swollen and soft – this recipe is the very definition of one-pot cooking. Serve in the pot at the table, or in bowls to eat on your knees – camping is as camping does, and all you'll have to wash up is the one pot, and a few bowls and forks.

2 tbsp good olive oil
4 chorizo sausages, thickly sliced
1 large onion, finely chopped
1 red (bell) pepper, deseeded and finely chopped
10 garlic cloves, peeled but whole
2 tsp sweet or hot, smoked or unsmoked paprika
just under ½ carton of tomato passata or ½ can of chopped tomatoes (200g/7oz)

1 tbsp tomato purée
4 cupfuls chicken or vegetable stock, or water (about 1 litre/35fl oz)
1²/₃ cupfuls paella rice (about 360g/12½oz)
about 1 cupful frozen peas (about 150g/5½oz)
salt and black pepper
1 lemon, cut into wedges, to serve

Heat the oil in a saucepan over a moderate heat. When hot, cook the chorizo for around 2 minutes, until lightly coloured and some of the fat has rendered into the pan. Add the onion, (bell) pepper, garlic and salt to taste and cook for about 10 minutes, until soft.

Stir in the paprika, passata or tomatoes and tomato purée and cook for 5–10 minutes, until rich and thickened.

Add the stock or water, then bring to the boil, adding extra salt to taste, if necessary, then add the rice and stir. Scatter over the peas and put a lid on the pan. Cook for 18–20 minutes, until the rice is tender, and most of the liquid has been absorbed.

Remove the rice from the heat and allow to rest with the lid on for at least 10 minutes before serving in bowls with the lemon wedges.

Spaghetti with sardines, chilli and fennel seeds

Tinned sardines are much underrated. Packed with omega-3 (good fats), they are nutritionally supercharged, but they also deliver flavour – and not just any old flavour, but deeply satisfying, bang-for-your-buck flavour. Plus, they are cheap to buy and easy to store. When you cook up this simple spaghetti with lemon, garlic and fennel seeds, you won't regret bringing the slender cans on your camping trip.

400g (14oz) spaghetti
3 x 120g (4¼oz) cans of sardine fillets
  in olive oil
1 tbsp good olive oil
1–2 garlic cloves, finely chopped or
  sliced

½–1 tsp dried chilli flakes, to taste, plus
  more to serve
2 tsp fennel seeds
1 lemon, halved
salt and black pepper

Cook the pasta in well-salted water for 10–12 minutes, or according to the packet instructions, until al dente. Drain, reserving some of the cooking water. Set aside and dry the saucepan.

Open the tin of sardines and add the oil in the tin to the saucepan along with the tablespoon of olive oil. Place over a moderate heat and add the garlic, chilli and fennel, then cook for a couple of minutes, until fragrant. Remove from the heat.

Add the sardines and stir to warm through, then add the cooked spaghetti, mixing well. Season with black pepper and salt to taste, and add a squeeze of lemon juice. Serve immediately with extra chilli flakes if you like.

Frying pan calzone with mozzarella and chilli

Calzone is a pizza that has been folded into the shape of a half moon and cooked. Making fresh dough for pizza on a camping trip, while entirely doable, is a step too far for many, I feel. In which case, buy good-quality naan bread or Italian-style, sturdy flat breads for this recipe – shop-bought tortilla wraps are too thin. You want a bit of puff; enough doughy-ness to fold and ape a pizza crust. The result is a short-cut calzone with dough that takes enough time to melt the mozzarella and soften the tomatoes a little. You could call this a toasted sandwich... you could, but I'm not going to.

1–2 tbsp good olive oil
2 cupfuls cherry tomatoes (about 250g/9oz)
big pinch of salt
4 large flat breads or sturdy wraps

2 x 125g (4½oz) balls of mozzarella, drained, then roughly chopped and patted dry
dried oregano, to taste
dried chilli flakes, to taste

Heat the olive oil in a frying pan over a moderate heat. Add the tomatoes and big pinch of salt and cook for 3–5 minutes, until the tomatoes have softened but still hold a little of their shape. Remove from the heat, drain and set the tomatoes aside. Wipe out the pan, ready to cook the calzone.

Lay out each flat bread on a clean surface. Distribute the cooked tomatoes, mozzarella, oregano and chilli flakes equally over each flat bread, leaving a good border of at least a couple of centimetres (an inch) around the edge to prevent anything seeping out when you fry. Fold each flat bread over in half to create a half moon shape.

Working in batches, in a dry frying pan, fry each flat bread over a moderate–low heat, for about 3 minutes on the first side, until the bread on the underside takes on a nice colour, is even blistered in places, and the mozzarella has melted sufficiently. Flip over the calzone and cook on the other side for another 3 minutes.

Remove from the heat and cut into quarters to serve.

Cornbread toad-in-the-hole

You need an oven for 'real' toad-in-the-hole, but this recipe uses fine polenta and cooks the dish like a corn bread, flipping it in the pan to bronze, cook and crisp on each side. Cook the sausages in the pan first, then make the corn-bread batter, pouring it into the hot pan, before arranging the sausages. Use a good non-stick or cast-iron pan and get it very hot to prevent the corn batter from sticking. We like to eat this warm with tomato ketchup or chilli sauce. It's best eaten on the day it is made – cornbread tends to dry out if left overnight.

½ cupful fine-ground polenta (about 95g/3½oz)

½ cupful (about 75g/2½oz) self-raising (self-rising) flour

1 tbsp caster (superfine) sugar

¾ tsp fine salt

½ tsp baking powder

½ tub or 1 cupful full-fat natural yogurt (about 260g/9½oz), thinned with a little milk; or use buttermilk

2 large eggs

2 tbsp butter, plus more for 'baking' the toad

14 thin sausages or chipolatas

favourite sauce, to serve

4 fried eggs, to serve (optional)

Whisk the polenta, flour, sugar, salt and baking powder together in a large bowl. Add the yogurt and eggs and mix briefly to combine (don't overwork the mixture from now on).

Place a large cast-iron or non-stick pan over a high heat, then add the butter and heat until melted and foaming. Add the sausages and cook, turning occasionally, for about 5 minutes, until browned all over. Transfer the sausages to a large plate.

Ensure the heat is high, add any fat in the pan to the batter in the bowl, swirling it through briefly, then add a good-size knob more of butter to the pan to sizzle and foam. Pour the batter into the pan and arrange the sausages on top in an even layer. Cover tightly with a lid or foil, reduce the heat to medium and cook undisturbed for 7–10 minutes, until the batter is firm and hot throughout and slightly puffed, and the base is golden brown.

Remove from the heat and invert the toad-in-the-hole onto a plate. Return the pan to the heat and carefully slide the toad back into the pan to colour for 3–5 minutes, until cooked and golden brown on the top and bottom.

Cut into wedges and serve immediately with your favourite sauce and a fried egg, if you like.

Béchamel cheese cheat's fondue

Cheese fondue is a wonderful thing, but camping in pared-down, more alfresco dining environments can make a warm and oozy fondue somewhat challenging. So, I'm suggesting you make a thick béchamel sauce and then add plenty of cheese. I like a mixture of Comté, Emmental and Gruyère, for their varied ages and styles that give different melting characteristics to the finished sauce. Choosing what to serve with fondue is all part of the fun – good crusty bread is non-negotiable, likewise boiled small potatoes, and pickles. Charcuterie and chunky slices of apple are also good. If the fondue does begin to thicken as it cools, simply return the pan to the heat and warm through – the roux in the béchamel will prevent the cheese from splitting.

1¾ cupfuls whole milk (about 400ml/14fl oz)

2 garlic cloves, unpeeled and smashed

2 tbsp plain (all-purpose) flour (about 20g/¾oz)

3 tbsp butter

1 cupful grated Gruyère (about 100g/3½oz)

1 cupful cubed raclette (about 100g/3½oz)

1 cupful grated Cheddar (about 100g/3½oz)

salt and black pepper

TO SERVE

2 crusty baguettes, cut into rough cubes, to serve

400g (14oz) boiled new potatoes, cut into quarters lengthways

various pickles, such as cornichons, to serve

Pour the milk into a saucepan and add the garlic cloves. Heat over medium heat until it just starts to boil, then pour it into a heatproof jug and set to one side.

In the same pan, this time over low heat, whisk together the flour and butter to form a roux, stirring briskly for 2–3 minutes, until the mixture begins to fur the bottom of the pan and the flour is cooked out. In a steady stream, add the warm milk, whisking continuously as the béchamel begins to thicken. Turn the heat up to medium and cook the sauce for at least 5 minutes, stirring all the time, until thickened and smooth.

Turn the heat back down to low and begin adding the cheeses, one handful at a time, whisking until each addition is melted and fully incorporated before adding another. Repeat the process until all the cheese is in and the sauce is thick and glossy. Check the seasoning, adding salt and black pepper to taste. Remove from the heat and serve warm with the bread, potatoes, pickles and so on.

Honey and paprika chicken with fried potatoes

The considerable honey and paprika in this recipe make the chicken incredibly fragrant and delicious as it cooks down in the tomato sauce. I'm suggesting serving this one-pot chicken dish with some fried potatoes – taking the overall pan count up to two. If you are cooking with just the one pan, you might want to consider serving crusty bread to mop instead of cooking the potatoes. But if you're in a leisurely mood, fry the potatoes first, wipe out the pan, and keep the cooked potatoes to one side (an ambient temperature is fine), before embarking on the chicken, then serving the two together.

8 skin-on, bone-in chicken thighs
olive oil, to fry
2 garlic bulbs, halved horizontally
1 onion, halved horizontally
1 tbsp sweet or hot paprika, smoked or unsmoked, plus extra for sprinkling the potatoes
2 tbsp runny honey

400g (14oz) tomato passata or can of chopped tomatoes
salt and black pepper

FOR THE FRIED POTATOES (TO SERVE)
16 new potatoes, halved
olive oil, to fry

First, make the fried potatoes. Bring a pan of salted water to the boil over a high heat, then boil for about 10 minutes, until cooked through. Drain. Heat a splash of olive oil in a frying pan over a moderate–low heat and fry for 10–15 minutes, turning occasionally, until golden brown all over. Sprinkle with paprika, transfer to a plate and set aside.

Season the chicken with a good amount of salt. Heat a splash of olive oil in a saucepan over a moderate heat and add the chicken, frying and turning for 5–8 minutes per side, until golden brown all over.

Add the garlic and onion, cut-sides down, to the pan and cook for 5 minutes, until both have turned golden, then stir in the paprika and honey and cook for a few seconds more. Add the passata or tomatoes and simmer for 8–10 minutes, until well reduced, rich and thickened.

Finally, add enough water to barely cover the chicken, then put a lid on the pan. Turn the heat down to low and cook very gently for 40–45 minutes, or until the chicken is very tender and almost falling off the bone.

Remove from the heat, check the seasoning and season to taste with extra salt and plenty of black pepper, as necessary, to serve with the potatoes.

3

FIRESIDE COOKING

Cooking over fire is primal. The fire bewitches and captivates; it is a source of heat to cook on, warmth to sit beside and light to illuminate. It is everything and more. It is, in essence, what we all consider to be the true experience of cooking outdoors. The recipes in this chapter are all fairly easy to assemble. They exhort the use of the camper van storecupboard, backed up with an assortment of fire-friendly ingredients. This is food that likes the lick of a flame, or to sit wrapped in foil in the glowing embers or on a grill over a red-hot heat. There's a burger recipe, of course, but this recipe includes harissa, also halloumi, both of which act as essential and easy seasoning boosts to the quantity of mince (ground meat). Throughout the chapter I've tried to list ingredients that are easy to stockpile for a forthcoming camping trip, leaving you with just the fresh produce to source nearer the time; or, better still, on location. I'm talking fish mostly, but good meat from local farm shops or butchers, too. Also, I am always one to roam about the countryside with beady eyes peeled, looking out for any home-grown produce. I love the vegetable stands you see in rural locations complete with honesty boxes for payment.

For the purposes of cooking outdoors, we have a humongous fire grill or *chapa*, which is an Argentinian-style fire grid or flat plate on which a grill, and sometimes a solid top, stands over the heat source. It's very effective and also works almost as a fire table, radiating heat, with the odd extra log then chucked on. It keeps us warm long after cooking. We also have a little pot-bellied stove into which you feed charcoal, placing the little grill or solid top above the source of heat. You use the charcoal stove much as you would a gas or electric hob on a domestic oven, but with the added, and frankly gorgeous, aroma that is proper charcoal. Oh, and not forgetting the massive great beast that is a simple bonfire, built to burn on the ground, feeding the fiery mass logs and sticks and using the raw inferno to warm your party as night falls, and also as a source of heat for cooking. The only thing to mention here is that free-form fires, such as a bonfire, can scorch the ground, and sparks can spread quickly with no barrier to contain the flames, creating a wildfire hazard. For these reasons, some campsites won't allow them. Personally, I think it best to use a fire box or plate as the fire is easier to contain, and the construction leaves less room for error and gives you peace of mind when all is done and it's time to go to bed.

Steak sandwich with cream cheese and 'nduja

The premise here is to buy one large bavette steak, season it well, and then cook it as a whole piece over a fierce heat. Keep it rare because bavette likes a lean cooking time, and rest it as long as is sensible before slicing and stuffing a tangle of juicy steak into a crusty baguette, slathered with 'nduja and cream cheese. Cooking some onions with the steak is an unbeatable combination. This is the steak-sandwich hill on which I am prepared to die, or at the very least lie down.

2 garlic cloves, crushed
1 tsp dried oregano
2 tbsp olive oil
2 tbsp red wine vinegar
600–800g (1lb 5oz–1lb 12oz) bavette steak or other favourite cut
1 red onion, thinly sliced
salt and black pepper

TO SERVE
4 large crusty rolls (the bigger the better), split open but not sliced all the way through
200g (7oz) full-fat cream cheese
3 generous tablespoons 'nduja

In a large bowl, mix together the garlic, oregano, and 1 tablespoon each of the olive oil and vinegar. Season generously with pepper. Add the steak and leave it like this for a few hours, ideally. When you're ready to grill, season the meat well with salt.

I like to cook the steak as a whole piece, rest it, then slice it to share. This means cooking it over a very hot grill for 2–3 minutes, then flipping it and cooking the other side for 2–3 minutes. Then, move the steak to a cooler part of the grill, flip it again and cook it for another 1–2 minutes, then repeat on the other side. Remove the steak from the grill and rest it on a plate for at least 10–15 minutes somewhere warm. While the steak is resting prepare the onions.

In a pan over a high heat, fry the onion in the remaining olive oil for about 5 minutes (turning brown is good), then add the remaining vinegar and cook over a high heat, until the vinegar has fully evaporated. Season to taste.

When you are ready to slice the steak, spread the bread rolls with the 'nduja and cream cheese. Add the fried onions and put to one side ready for the steak.

Slice the steak against the grain into ribbons. The fatter side should be rare and juicy with the thinner side slightly more well-cooked, so that everyone can enjoy it to their liking. Add the sliced steak to the prepared rolls and serve immediately.

Fried mackerel with horseradish butter, gherkins and lettuce in brioche buns

My 13-year-old daughter Grace cooked the mackerel in this shot for this book. I'm all for giving children a bit of freedom to cook, and camping is as good an opportunity as any. Mackerel is a splendid, oily fish for kids to have a go at, because it is fairly forgiving. You can grill the fillets with their skin on (or use a pan), and because they are slim, they take just minutes to cook. Mackerel has a beautiful texture, and especially so if the skin crisps and chars in places as it cooks. In this recipe, I've served them with gherkins and soft lettuce, on buttered brioche rolls with a spoonful of horseradish. Eat these buns on the beach – you won't regret it.

4 tbsp butter, softened
2–4 tbsp horseradish, to taste
4 large or 8 small mackerel fillets
1 soft round lettuce, leaves separated
4 large gherkins, sliced
salt and black pepper
4 brioche buns (or any soft roll), split
    open, to serve

Beat the butter and horseradish together in a bowl, adding pepper to taste, then put the mixture to one side.

Season the mackerel fillets on both sides and grill them over a high heat, skin-side down, for 2 minutes. Carefully flip the fillets over with a spatula and cook for another 1 minute, until just cooked through. (Cook in a pan with a splash of cooking oil, if you prefer.)

Lightly toast the inside of the rolls on the grill, then generously spread each with the horseradish butter. Add lettuce and gherkins to each bun, then finally the cooked mackerel, sandwiching shut to serve.

Halloumi, potato and jalapeño skewers with sour cream

Skewers are sensible barbecue and camping tools because – stating the obvious here – they keep everything in place when cooking over a fire. Hot off the grill and doused with sour cream, this is a wonderful recipe. I've cut the lemon into quarters and grilled it along with the halloumi skewers because blistered, hot-grilled lemons are magic, and super-juicy. You'll need wooden or metal skewers for this recipe – if you're using wooden, soak them in a little water for 30 minutes before threading.

2 x 225g (8oz) packets of halloumi (about 2 packets), cut into 3cm (1¼in) cubes

500g (1lb 2oz) baby new potatoes, boiled until tender

2 jalapeño chillies (or other green chilli), cut into 6 pieces (deseeded if you want less heat)

1 large red onion, cut into 6 wedges

3 tbsp olive oil, plus more to serve

1 tsp sweet or hot, smoked or unsmoked paprika

1 lemon, quartered

150g (5½oz) sour cream (1 small tub)

salt and black pepper

chilli flakes, to serve

In a bowl, toss together the halloumi, cooked potatoes, jalapeños and onion in the olive oil, paprika and juice from two of the lemon quarters. Season with salt and pepper (remembering the halloumi is salty).

Thread everything in equal proportions onto the skewers. Grill over a moderate–high heat for about 5 minutes, turning every so often, until everything is golden and lightly charred.

At the same time, grill the remaining lemon quarters, cut-side down, until charred and juicy.

Season the sour cream to taste with a good pinch of salt and put to one side in a bowl.

Remove the skewers from the grill and drizzle with the sour cream. Trickle over a splash more olive oil and juice from the grilled lemon quarters, then sprinkle with chilli flakes to serve.

Peppers, aubergines, onions and courgettes cooked in foil with feta cheese

Ratatouille, sort of. Better still, the Spanish dish of *escalivada*, which is traditionally cooked in the embers of the fire from the night before to eat the following day. Slicing all the vegetables and wrapping them in foil to bake in the embers is super-easy as far as camping cooking goes, giving you enough time to make a good, rich tomato sauce, flavoured with dried oregano, into which you can then heave all the softened, steamed-in-their-own-juices vegetables and scatter with a good amount of feta. Chilli flakes, good olive oil and some crusty bread wouldn't go amiss to serve.

2 onions, very thinly sliced
1 large aubergine (eggplant), halved
  lengthways, sliced into 1cm (½in)
  half moons
4 courgettes (zucchini), sliced into 1cm
  (½in) rounds
2 red (bell) peppers, deseeded and
  quartered
4 garlic cloves, very thinly sliced

1 x 400g (14oz) can of chopped
  tomatoes
1 tsp dried oregano
generous amount of olive oil
salt and black pepper
1 x 200g (7oz) packet of feta, crumbled,
  to serve

Preheat the grill or barbecue to hot, or use the red-hot embers of the fire.

One kind at a time, toss the prepared vegetables each in about 2 tablespoons of olive oil and season with salt and pepper. Get 4 squares of heavy-duty foil, or use a double layer of standard foil, and wrap each type of chopped vegetable – the onions, courgettes (zucchini), aubergine (eggplant) and (bell) peppers – in a loose-fitting but well-sealed parcel.

Place the parcels directly into a moderate–low heat source, in the embers or at the edges of a grill or barbecue, and cook for 25–30 minutes, until the vegetables are completely tender – the aubergine should need the longest (you might need an extra 10 minutes or so).

Meanwhile, cook the garlic in a pan with 2 tablespoons of olive oil over a moderate heat for 2 minutes, then add the tomatoes and oregano and cook for 10–15 minutes, until rich and thick. Season to taste with salt and plenty of black pepper.

With the vegetables all cooked, unwrap the parcels, tip them into the hot sauce and mix well, adding the feta and a slick more olive oil to serve.

Baked potatoes stuffed with soft garlic cheese, spring onions and bacon

There's something deeply satisfying about wrapping potatoes in foil, then cooking the parcels in the embers of the fire – steaming, baking – until they are soft and cooked through. Precious little effort required. The second bake – of stuffing and re-sealing, then putting the potatoes back in the embers to heat through for the cheese to soften and ooze – is nothing but a bonus. Choose sensibly sized potatoes, nothing enormous, as these will take an age to cook.

4 medium baking potatoes
8 rashers of streaky bacon
olive oil
4 spring onions (scallions), trimmed
  and thinly sliced
salt and black pepper
300g (10½oz) garlic and herb soft
  cheese (2 packs)

Pierce the potatoes all over with a fork or sharp knife – you will need to do this or they might explode in the fire.

Wrap each potato in foil and arrange in the fire or barbecue embers and cook for about 1 hour–1 hour 30 minutes, turning every 20 minutes, until completely tender.

Meanwhile, cook the bacon in a pan or on the grill until crisp and golden. Put to one side.

Toward the final 15 minutes of the potatoes' cooking time, unseal the parcels, still keeping the underside of each potato in the foil, and add a good pinch of salt and a drizzle of olive oil. With the foil still loosened, continue cooking for a further 15 or so minutes, to allow the potato skins to crisp a little.

Cut a deep cross into each potato and squeeze open. Add the bacon, soft cheese and spring onions (scallions), loosely seal in the foil once more and pop the potato back in the heat source for 5–10 minutes for the cheese to soften and melt and the bacon to warm up. Serve immediately.

Fish and prawn parcels cooked with cherry tomatoes and fresh chilli

Frozen prawns (shrimp) are an excellent item to take camping as they can defrost en route and will bump up the flavour in this recipe. Buy firm, flat fish fillets such as plaice or bream for this recipe. You will need a hot grill or barbecue or you can use the red-hot embers of a fire. You need to leave a good amount of space for hot air to circulate within the parcels as the fish cooks, so don't compress the foil too much, but be sure to seal the edges tightly so no juices can escape. Serve with good bread to mop up the juices, or buttered boiled potatoes. An extra slick of good olive oil on the fish to serve is never a bad thing.

2 garlic cloves, very thinly sliced
1 small onion, very thinly sliced
20 cherry tomatoes, halved
1 red chilli, finely chopped (deseeded if you want less heat; optional) or more if you like
1 lemon or orange, 4 large strips of zest removed (without pith)
12–16 raw prawns (shrimp), defrosted and peeled (optional)

800g (1lb 12oz) firm flat fish fillets (such as bream or plaice), skin off if you prefer
good-size knob of butter
salt and black pepper
crusty bread, or boiled and buttered potatoes, to serve

Lay out 4 sheets of foil lengthways and divide the garlic, onion, tomatoes, chilli (if using) and citrus zest in the middle of each piece.

Divide the prawns (shrimp; if using) and the fish fillets between the parcels, placing them on top of the tomatoes. Divide the butter among the parcels and season well with salt and pepper.

Seal the foil, folding all sides inwards to create an airtight parcel. Don't make it too compressed, ideally you want a little air to circulate within.

Carefully place the parcels on the barbecue or in the red-hot embers and cook for 13–16 minutes, until the parcels have puffed up and are very hot to touch.

Remove the parcels from the heat and allow the fish to rest, still sealed, for a minute or so, then place the parcels onto plates to serve, taking care when opening the foil seal as the steam and juices will be very hot.

Fish tandoori with mango raita and cucumber

Choose firm white fish from a sustainable source and marinate the lot in a mixture of yogurt, ginger, garlic and dried spices (the marinade is also terrific on chicken or lamb). Use a cage to grill the fish, if you have one, to keep the pieces in place as they cook. Alternatively, skewer the marinated fish and grill as a kebab until cooked. Over fire is best for tandoori – the marinade likes a red-hot heat, but you could cook this in a pan over a camping stove if you needed to. Buy good-quality mango chutney and mix it through with yogurt for an easy, punchy raita. You could assemble this blend of spices at home to take with you as a ready-made tandoori spice blend.

800g–1kg (1lb 12oz–2lb 4oz) firm white fish fillets (such as monkfish), cut into bite-size pieces (about 2.5cm/1in)

FOR THE TANDOORI MARINADE
1 tbsp Kashmiri chilli powder, or use 1 tsp chilli powder and 1 tsp sweet or hot, smoked or unsmoked paprika
1 tsp ground turmeric
2 tsp ground cumin
1 tsp ground coriander
½ tsp ground cinnamon
½ tsp ground fennel seeds
½ tsp black pepper
generous ½ cup full-fat natural yogurt (about 150g/5½oz)

1 tbsp grated fresh ginger
2 garlic cloves, crushed
1 tsp salt
pinch of caster (superfine) sugar

TO SERVE
1 heaped tbsp full-fat natural yogurt per person or flat bread
1 heaped tsp mango chutney per person or flat bread
big pinch of salt
1–2 chapati, roti, naan, or any flat breads per person
1 cucumber, thinly sliced
green chilli, thinly sliced (optional; deseeded if you want less heat)

Mix all the marinade ingredients together in a bowl and add the fish, mixing well to coat. Then, ideally, marinate somewhere cool for 30 minutes–1 hour.

Over a hot grill or barbecue, cook the fish, turning often, on skewers or in a cage, for 5–8 minutes, or until lightly charred and cooked through.

Meanwhile, mix together the yogurt with the mango chutney and salt in a small bowl. Put to one side.

Briefly heat the flat breads on the grill before adding equal amounts of the cooked fish to each and spooning over the mango raita, sliced cucumber and sliced chilli (if using), to serve.

Piri piri chicken with corn-on-the-cob and roasted sweet potato

Fiery, spicy chargrilled chicken is always a popular choice. A dish with Portuguese, and by proxy East African roots, piri piri is easy to make but does rely on a liberal, brave use of red-hot chillies – searingly hot pili pili ones for authenticity. If you can't find them then bird's eye or scotch bonnet will do the trick, and so would a regular red chilli, although you may want to double or even triple the quantity. The outcome must be hot, hot, hot – lip-smackingly so. I've served the chicken with roasted corn and sweet potato, but chips or rice will also work; even good-quality crisps would do.

1–3 tsp chilli flakes
6 garlic cloves, peeled and crushed
1 tsp dried oregano
2 tsp sweet or hot, smoked or
  unsmoked paprika
5 tbsp olive oil
3 tbsp red or white wine vinegar
juice of 1 large lemon or 2 limes
8 chicken thighs (skin removed, if you
  prefer), or use wings or legs
salt and black pepper

TO SERVE
4 small sweet potatoes
4 corn-on-the-cobs, boiled for
  5 minutes, then drained

In a mixing bowl combine the chilli flakes, garlic, oregano, paprika, olive oil, vinegar and citrus juice, adding plenty of salt and black pepper taste. Divide into two – one portion to use as a marinade and one to use as a sauce for the cooked chicken.

Season the chicken thighs with salt, then coat each piece of chicken in the piri piri marinade, ideally leaving the thighs in the marinade for about 30 minutes, or more, if you can keep them refrigerated.

Meanwhile, loosely wrap the sweet potatoes in foil and place them in the embers of the fire to bake for about 30 minutes, until soft and fudgy.

Grill the chicken over a moderate–high heat for 10–12 minutes on each side, depending on the size of the thighs, turning from time to time and using any leftover marinade to baste the thighs as they cook on the grill. Ideally the chicken will be a little charred in places when cooked through.

While the chicken is cooking, grill the blanched corn, turning often and basting it with any remaining marinade, until charred all over.

Serve the chicken with the corn and the sweet potatoes and the reserved portion of piri piri sauce on the side.

Meatballs with butter beans and jarred pepper paste

Serve these meatballs in toasted pita, scooping them into the warm breads with beans, a dollop of Greek yogurt, a pinch of chilli flakes and some hot sauce. You will need a suitable pan to cook the pepper paste with the onions and meatballs over the fire or barbecue. You could also make this recipe on a camping gas ring, but I do think a bit of flame and smoke on the meatballs as they bronze will complement the beans. I buy Turkish pepper paste from my local Middle Eastern corner store, but it is also available online and, once opened, will keep for up to four weeks in the fridge. It delivers a lot of flavour per spoonful and is a terrific camping storecupboard ingredient.

450g (1lb) minced (ground) beef
  or lamb
1 egg, beaten
1 onion, very finely chopped
1 tsp dried oregano
1 tsp ground cumin
½ tsp salt, or more to taste
½ tsp black pepper, or more to taste
6 garlic cloves, finely chopped
3 tbsp olive oil, plus more to serve
3 tbsp jarred pepper paste, or use a

paste made from 2 tsp sweet smoked
  or unsmoked paprika and 2 tbsp
  tomato purée with a splash of water
2 x 400g (14oz) cans butter (lima)
  beans, drained

TO SERVE
flat breads or pita breads, toasted
generous ½ cup full-fat Greek yogurt
  (about 150g/5½oz)
chilli flakes or hot chilli sauce (optional)

Mix together the minced (ground) meat, egg and half the chopped onion, with the oregano, cumin, salt and pepper, then divide evenly and shape the meat into walnut-sized meatballs.

Heat the olive oil in a frying pan over a moderate heat and cook the remaining onion and the garlic for 8–10 minutes, until soft and translucent and beginning to brown a little.

Meanwhile grill the meatballs until they are browned on all sides – 5–8 minutes. Or, if you have space for just 1 pan, when the onions are ready, scoop them out onto a plate, put the meatballs into the pan and brown them on the heat.

Add the meatballs to the pan with the onions (or add the onions back to the pan), then add the pepper paste and butter (lima) beans, mixing well. Add just enough water to cover the meatballs, then cook, uncovered, on a moderate–low heat for about 20 minutes, or until the meat is cooked through and the sauce is rich and thickened. Check the seasoning, adding more salt and pepper to taste, if necessary.

Remove the pan from the heat and serve the meatballs in the toasted pitas, with the yogurt and the chilli flakes or hot chilli sauce (if using) to dollop on the side.

Beef burger with halloumi and harissa mayonnaise

Because there *had* to be a burger (and adding halloumi and harissa can only be a good thing)... Cook the burger pink, resting it well while you fry the halloumi and assemble the bun. Harissa and halloumi are great camping ingredients – both with a good shelf life and both packing a punch in terms of flavour and texture. Cook this over a grill or pan fry – but both the burger and the cheese do like the lick of a grill flame. Try to use minced (ground) meat with a high fat content – all the juicier! The recipe works well with either beef or lamb.

FOR THE BURGERS
600g (1lb 5oz) minced (ground) beef
   or lamb
1 red onion, ½ grated, ½ thinly sliced
1 garlic clove, crushed (optional)
½ tsp salt, plus extra for the sliced
   onion
boiling water
black pepper

FOR THE HARISSA MAYONNAISE
1–2 tbsp harissa
4 tbsp mayonnaise or full-fat
   Greek yogurt

TO ASSEMBLE
1 x 225g (8oz) packet of halloumi,
   drained and sliced into 4
4 brioche buns, halved and toasted
   a little on the grill
8–12 lettuce leaves
2 ripe tomatoes, sliced

Make the burgers. Combine the minced (ground) meat, grated onion, garlic (if using) and the salt in a large bowl and mix very well, kneading a bit to soften. Divide the mince into 4 equal pieces and shape each into a burger about 1cm (½in) wider than the brioche buns. Set aside, ideally for 30 minutes, to let the flavours mingle.

Make the harissa mayonnaise by combining all the ingredients in a bowl. Set aside. Pour boiling water over the thinly sliced onion, drain, then transfer to a small bowl and season with a big pinch of salt. Set aside.

Grill the burgers for 2–3 minutes on each side, until bronzed on the outside and still juicy in the middle. Remove from the grill and leave to rest while you grill the halloumi for about 30 seconds on each side, until nicely coloured. Remove from the heat.

Build the burgers on the buns adding with the lettuce, harissa mayonnaise, halloumi, sliced onion and tomato.

Pork kebabs with tzatziki, sliced tomato and flat breads

The marinade in this recipe is great and will work just as well for chicken or lamb. It gives this kebab a good, juicy jump-start. I'm grilling the lemons, because this way they really are unbeatable when squeezed over to serve. Many of these camping recipes rely on bread as a serving suggestion – it's ambient, no-cook and easy to serve campside, and of course comes in gluten-free alternatives. You'll need wooden or metal skewers for this recipe – if you're using wooden, soak them in a little water for 30 minutes before threading.

1 lemon, zested then quartered
1 tsp dried oregano
1 tsp sweet paprika
2 garlic cloves, crushed
3 tbsp olive oil
800g (1lb 12oz) pork leg, loin or fillet, cut into 3–4cm (1¼–1½in) dice
salt and black pepper
4 large flat breads or pita breads, toasted, to serve
4 ripe tomatoes, sliced, to serve

FOR THE TZATZIKI
½ cucumber, peeled, deseeded and coarsely grated
generous 1 cup full-fat Greek yogurt (about 250g/9oz)
½ tsp dried mint (optional)
1 garlic clove, crushed

In a bowl, mix together lemon zest and half the juice with the oregano, paprika, garlic, olive oil and diced pork. Leave to marinate for at least 30 minutes, and up to 8 hours if refrigerated.

Strain the pork, reserving the marinade, and thread the meat equally onto the skewers. Set aside.

Make the tzatziki. Give the grated cucumber a good squeeze to extract as much liquid as you can, then put it in a bowl with the yogurt. Season generously with salt, then add the dried mint if using, and the remaining crushed garlic, mixing well to combine. Set aside.

Place the skewers over a hot grill or barbecue for 8–10 minutes altogether, basting with the reserved marinade as the kebabs cook and turning halfway through the cooking time, until the pork is cooked through. Grill the remaining lemon wedges, too, if you like, until charred and juicy.

Remove the skewers from the heat when the pork is ready and assemble the flat breads, filling them with the grilled pork, sliced tomato and a big dollop of tzatziki, and using the grilled lemon wedges to squeeze all over.

Chicken satay with prawn crackers and cucumber

Ideally, you'll marinate your chicken in quite a bit of chilli before grilling, making the pieces just on the right side of fiery for dipping, cooked, into the smooth peanut sauce. This is a dish of opposite forces, with the heat of the chilli tempered by the sweet, creamy peanut. Both pair beautifully with the salty prawn crackers and juicy, cool cucumber. Do try to get hold of some kecap manis; it has great shelf life for the camping storecupboard. I could eat this for breakfast, lunch and dinner. It is the perfect camping meal.

You'll need metal or wooden skewers for this recipe – if you're using wooden, soak them in a little water for 30 minutes before threading.

½–2 tsp (or more) chilli powder or
  flakes, to taste
2 tsp ground coriander
4 tbsp kecap manis (or soy sauce mixed
  with ½ tsp sugar per 1 tbsp of soy),
  plus more if needed
600g (1lb 5oz) skinless chicken fillets,
  cut into 3cm (1¼in) dice
200g (7oz) full-fat coconut milk
  (a standard pouch)
1 tsp fish sauce

about ½ jar of smooth unsweetened
  peanut butter
1 lime, quartered
salt and black pepper

TO SERVE
prawn crackers, lots and lots, at least
  a couple of big bags
1 cucumber, sliced in rounds

Mix the chilli powder or flakes, coriander, plenty of black pepper and half the kecap manis together in a bowl with the chicken and leave to marinate for as long as possible – throughout the day, overnight, or for a couple of hours, any which way, just as long as it will keep cold.

Using a fork, whisk the remaining kecap manis with the coconut milk and fish sauce in a small saucepan over a moderate–low heat until warm. Add the peanut butter, whisking to combine to a smooth sauce. Remove from the heat, then mix in the juice from two of the lime quarters. Check the seasoning and adjust with extra salt and kecap manis, if necessary. (You might also like to add a little hot water, whisking to combine, to thin the sauce if the peanut butter is in need of loosening.) Put to one side, somewhere warm.

Thread the marinated chicken onto the skewers and barbecue or grill them over a moderate–high heat until the surface is nicely caramelized and the chicken is cooked through (around 8–10 minutes), turning often. You can also pan fry these if you like, but I like to see a bit of char on satay. Remove from the heat.

Serve the skewers with the prawn crackers and cucumber slices, with the satay sauce to drizzle and dip and the remaining lime quarters on the side to squeeze.

Sausage hotdogs with fried sauerkraut and gherkin ketchup mayonnaise

This is quite possibly the best version of a hotdog you will ever eat, camping or otherwise. By all means adjust and use vegetarian sausages if you like – it's the combination of grilled hot dog jammed in a soft bun with cheese, fried sauerkraut and a punchy, piquant sauce that makes this recipe the success it really is. Sauerkraut is a perfect ingredient to take with you camping. It has a good shelf life and delivers instant flavour in a way that few vegetables really can, given the circumstances. In this recipe, it's fried briefly – caramelizing it just a little is incalculably good. You've been warned.

4 large good-quality sausages (high meat content with little or no rusk)
1 cupful drained sauerkraut (about 200g/7oz)
4 small handfuls of sliced or grated hard cheese, such as Cheddar
4 hotdog buns, split open

FOR THE MAYONNAISE
2 pickled gherkins, finely chopped
2 tbsp ketchup
4 tbsp mayonnaise
½ small onion or 1 shallot, very finely chopped
2 tbsp horseradish sauce
1 tbsp smooth, yellow mustard
salt and black pepper

Cook the sausages over a moderately hot grill for about 10 minutes, turning often, until cooked through.

Meanwhile, mix all of the dressing ingredients together in a bowl and season to taste with salt and pepper.

In a small frying pan, or directly on the grill plate, over a moderate heat, fry the sauerkraut until brown in places – 3–4 minutes should do.

Fill each hot dog bun with a small handful of cheese, wrap them in foil and place them onto the hot grill or in the embers of the fire. Warm them just enough to begin melting the cheese in the bun.

Remove the buns from the heat, unwrap them and insert the sausages on top of the melted cheese. Top with the sauerkraut and plenty of the dressing to serve.

Pork and pineapple skewers

Grilling the pineapple along with the marinated pork is transformative. This is the best sort of grilling or barbecuing – effortless and very, very tasty. Memorable are these skewers, all slathered with hot sauce and pink pickled onions. Hot juicy pork, sweet and spicy with chilli and honey served with grilled pineapple – there's no going back. Peaches or apricots would make brilliant alternatives to pineapple. You'll need metal or wooden skewers for this recipe – if you're using wooden, soak them in a little water for 30 minutes before threading.

1 tbsp soft light brown sugar or runny honey

1 tsp chilli powder (chipotle would be ideal)

½ tsp ground cumin

4 tbsp olive oil

½ tsp salt, plus more to season

½ tsp black pepper

600g (1lb 5oz) pork loin or fillet, cut into 2–3cm (¾–1¼in) pieces

1 red onion, ½ very thinly sliced, ½ cut into 4 wedges

boiling water

2 limes, halved

½–1 ripe pineapple, depending on size, cut into wedges, core removed, skin and stem intact

4 tortillas, to serve

your favourite hot sauce, to serve

In a large bowl, combine the brown sugar or honey, chilli powder, cumin, half the olive oil and the salt and pepper. Add the pork and onion wedges and mix well. Allow to marinate for at least 30 minutes, or more if refrigerated.

Place the sliced onion in a heatproof bowl and pour boiling water over it to cover. Drain, then add a big pinch of salt along with the juice of half a lime. Transfer to a small bowl and put to one side ready to serve.

Toss the pineapple in the remaining oil, then thread the pork and onion onto the skewers.

Grill the kebabs along with the wedges of pineapple, turning often, for 8–10 minutes, until the pork is cooked through and is nicely caramelized. The pineapple can come off the grill a little earlier than the pork if you like, but (like the pork) it likes a little bit of char, turning the flesh extra-juicy and flavoursome.

Remove the skewers from the grill. Let the pork rest for a couple of minutes, while you remove the skin and chop up the pineapple. Squeeze the juice from the remaining lime halves over the pork, then remove the pork and the onions from the skewers, piling the cooked pieces equally onto the tortillas with the chopped grilled pineapple, pickled onion and hot sauce to serve.

Lamb chops with cumin and sumac with tahini sauce

This combination is sensational. I like my chops still pink on the inside but with a good amount of charred and blistered skin and, importantly, the fat all glistening and crisp. So, do grill them hard and fast, then rest sufficiently for the chops to soften, turning melting and tender. You could serve these chops with rice, couscous or flat breads, whatever you find easiest to assemble fireside. I might suggest a chopped salad of cucumbers, red onions and tomato together with a big pinch of salt and a squeeze of lemon to accompany, which would be delicious.

2 garlic cloves, finely chopped
2 tsp ground cumin
1–2 tsp chilli flakes (aleppo or urfa is nice)
1 tbsp sumac
2 tbsp olive oil
12 lamb chops or cutlets
½ lemon (keep the other half for the sauce)
salt and black pepper

FOR THE TAHINI SAUCE
1 small garlic clove, crushed to a paste with a pinch of salt
3 tbsp tahini
juice of ½ lemon

TO SERVE
flat breads or pita breads, toasted, or cooked rice or couscous
pickles, to serve

In a bowl, mix the garlic, cumin, chilli flakes and half the sumac with the oil. Season the chops with salt and pepper, then rub the spiced oil into them and refrigerate them for at least 30 minutes before cooking.

Make the sauce. Combine the garlic and tahini in a bowl. Then, whisk or stir in the lemon juice and a splash of cold water to form a smooth sauce. The consistency should be like double cream. Season to taste with salt and pepper.

Heat a grill or large frying pan until very hot and cook the lamb chops briefly on one side until nicely coloured, then flip them over to cook on the other side. The cooking time should be between 2 and 5 minutes each side, depending on the thickness of the chops and how you like your lamb cooked. Grill the lemon half at the same time as the chops, until blistered and juicy. Remove the chops from the grill and rest for a couple of minutes. Remove the lemon and put to one side.

Serve the chops drizzled with the tahini sauce and sprinkled with the remaining sumac, using the grilled lemon half to liberally douse the chops with juice.

4

BREAKFAST AND BRUNCH

Mornings can be a little on the sluggish side when camping. So, first things first, get the kettle on – with a steaming cup of tea or coffee in hand, having to wait for breakfast, perhaps just a smidgen more than in any usual domestic setting, becomes 200% acceptable. If you have kids, I'd say it is a very wise thing to have a stash of favourite breakfast cereal within easy reach so that any of the younger (more hungry, or hangry – anyone?) people in your camping party can sate their hunger levels swiftly and efficiently; into a bowl, slosh of milk, spoon, go. (Worth noting here that I find oat milk a pretty good product for camping – it has longevity on its side and won't require refrigeration until opened.) All this will then give you plenty of time to assemble any of these recipes and will make you look so well skilled at campsite cookery, you'll easily get out of any washing-up duties – always a bonus, believe me. More coffee, anyone?

I find brunch to be such a civilized notion, and I'm going to suggest here that the only time people bother to factor in allowing the time for brunch in their lives is when they are camping, or on holiday, when time tends to take on a really curious quality. The days can revolve around the making and eating of food on repeat. These ten recipes cover the gambit of eating in the morning, through to late morning, even nearing lunchtime. Goodness – even anytime eating.

Porridge with banana, cinnamon and walnuts

We eat porridge regularly at home, but also while camping, possibly when we've got the kettle on to make tea first thing, when the kids are up and about and hungry. It gives us ample time to cajole any of the more sleepy party members before embarking on something more substantial, with coffee.

2 cupfuls whole or oat milk (about 500ml/17fl oz), plus more to serve
pinch of salt
1 cupful rolled oats (120g/4¼oz)
2 ripe bananas, thickly sliced
2 tbsp maple syrup or soft dark brown sugar

big pinch of ground cinnamon
4 tbsp chopped walnuts (or your favourite nut)
good-size knob of butter

Pour the milk into a medium saucepan with about a cupful of water (250ml/9fl oz) and the salt and bring to the boil over a moderate heat. Slowly whisk the oats into the boiling water to prevent any clumps and reduce the heat to low. Continue to cook, stirring occasionally, for 8–10 minutes, until the oats are plumped up and softened and the mixture is thick.

While the oats are cooking, mix the bananas, maple syrup and cinnamon together, and stir through the walnuts. Put to one side.

Serve the hot porridge in bowls, topped with a little of the butter and then the banana and walnut mixture.

BLT on muffin, BLEAT and BLAT too

This needs little introduction, although possibly the BLEAT and the BLAT need an explanation? The BLT is a sandwich with legendary status, and paramount are good tomatoes and crisp, juicy lettuce. Muffins make for a perfect vehicle as they are suitably soft and malleable, but still with enough structure and surface area to contain all the ingredients as one. Add avocados and you have a BLAT; add fried eggs, too, and you get a BLEAT. Simple, really.

FOR A BLT

1 tbsp sunflower or vegetable oil, or butter, plus more to cook the eggs (if BLEATing)

8 bacon rashers (streaky is best)

4 English muffins, split in half

4 tbsp mayonnaise

1 soft green lettuce or 2 little gems, leaves separated

4 ripe tomatoes, thinly sliced

ADD FOR A BLAT

2 ripe avocados, stoned, peeled and sliced

ADD FOR A BLEAT

4 eggs

Heat the oil or butter in a frying pan over a moderate heat. Add the bacon and cook to your liking – I like mine a bit crispy. Put the cooked bacon to one side and use the bacon fat in the pan to toast the muffins briefly, cut-side down, in the pan.

If you're making a BLEAT (or, I suppose, just a BLET), add some more oil or butter to the pan and cook the eggs to your liking, basting them with any leftover bacon fat in the pan.

Spread the mayonnaise over each muffin, add the bacon, tomato and lettuce, along with the avocado and egg, if using.

Yogurt pancakes

Smaller, fluffier-style pancakes, as opposed to thinner, lacier crêpes, are easier to cook when camping. You can also cook several in one pan at the same time, a hot tip for satisfying the impatient and the hungry. Some crisp bacon, drenched with maple syrup, is a classic match, but really, any of your favourite sweet-toast toppers will work wonders – fresh berries, sliced banana... you get the picture. Perhaps with an extra blob of yogurt, too.

just under 2 cupfuls self-raising (self-rising) flour (about 250g/9oz)
2 tbsp caster (superfine) sugar
pinch of salt
1 tub or about 2 cupfuls full-fat natural yogurt or buttermilk (about 500g/1lb 2oz)
2 eggs
4 tbsp butter, melted, or sunflower or vegetable oil

TO SERVE (ALL OPTIONAL)
crispy bacon
slices of banana
favourite berries
maple syrup, runny honey, chocolate spread or jam
extra yogurt

Mix together the flour, sugar and salt in a large bowl.

In a separate bowl, using a fork, whisk together the yogurt, eggs and half the melted butter (or oil) until smooth.

Using a spoon, mix the yogurt mixture into the dry ingredients until just combined, taking care not to over-mix, which will result in dense pancakes.

Spoon some of the remaining melted butter or oil into a frying pan over a moderate heat. Drop dessert-spoonfuls of the batter into the pan and cook each 'puddle' until the top side begins to bubble and the bottom turns golden brown. Flip the pancake and cook until the underside is golden brown – 1½–2 minutes per side should do. Remove from the heat and serve immediately with all the toppings on the side to choose from. Repeat with the remaining melted butter and batter, working in batches until everyone has a stack of pancakes.

Toasted waffles with grated dark chocolate and coconut yogurt

There are a good many versions of shop-bought waffles available and they are terrific to take camping. They have a long shelf life and make for a very speedy breakfast. If you have a fire going, by all means toast the waffles over a grill. Alternatively dry fry them in a pan over a camping stove until toasted and warmed through. The grated chocolate will melt obediently onto the hot waffles, which you then blob with the coconut yogurt. A great, easy combination for breakfast.

100g (3½oz) dark (bittersweet)
  or milk chocolate (a large bar),
  coarsely grated
8 waffles
about ¾ cupful coconut yogurt (about
  200g/7oz)

Divide the chocolate into 4 portions at the ready.

Toast the waffles, over a grill or in a dry frying pan over a moderate heat, until warm and golden. Transfer the waffles to 4 serving plates (2 waffles each).

Immediately sprinkle one of the portions of grated chocolate over each serving, repeating until all the waffles have a melty chocolate topping. Divide the coconut yogurt between the 4 servings and tuck in immediately.

Sweetcorn and halloumi fritters

I'm a fan of frozen sweetcorn over tinned, preferring the flavour and the texture. I've said it before – bags of frozen veg are a wonderful camping hack, providing extra refrigeration as they defrost along the way. Like the fluffy pancakes on page 127, fritters are a useful camping recipe. They are quick and easy to mix together in a bowl, and even easier to fry in batches sating all those waiting, and wailing, for breakfast. Serve with ketchup or your favourite chilli condiment.

1 heaped cupful self-raising
  (self-rising) flour (about 150g/5½oz)
3 eggs, beaten
5 tbsp whole milk
1 tsp chilli flakes
1 x 225g (8oz) packet of halloumi,
  coarsely grated
1 bunch of spring onions (scallions),
  trimmed and thinly sliced
2 cupfuls frozen sweetcorn, defrosted
  (about 300g/12oz)

sunflower or vegetable oil, for frying
salt and black pepper

TO SERVE
lemon or lime wedges
full-fat natural yogurt or sour cream
  mixed with a little salt to taste
your favourite hot sauce (optional)

Put the flour in a bowl. Whisk in the eggs, the milk, chilli flakes, halloumi, spring onions (scallions) and sweetcorn. Season with pepper and a bit of salt, remembering that the halloumi is quite salty.

In a large non-stick or cast-iron frying pan over a moderate heat, add enough oil to coat the bottom of the pan. When the pan is very hot, add tablespoonfuls of the batter and fry for 1–2 minutes – by which time the fritter should have formed. Flip to fry on the other side for a further 1–2 minutes, until cooked through. Work quickly in small batches until you have used up all the mixture.

Serve with lemon or lime wedges at the table with the seasoned yogurt and hot sauce, if using.

Hot-smoked salmon bagels with mustard butter and cream cheese

Smoked and kiln-roasted, hot-smoked salmon is already cooked when you buy it, has a better fridge life than fresh fish and just needs warming through to serve – all in all, vacuum-packed and stored in a cool bag (or camping fridge – get you!), it is a no-brainer camping ingredient. This is a delicious and elegant brunch. I think a wholemeal bagel is best, but white or sesame would work, too. I've used two mustards in equal amounts here, but doubling the quantity of just one would do.

5 tbsp butter, softened
2 tsp Dijon mustard
2 tsp wholegrain mustard
juice and finely grated zest of ½ lemon
1 small red onion, very thinly sliced
150g–200g (5½–7oz) hot-smoked
  salmon fillets, broken into bite-size
  chunks (or keep in fillets if slim)

4 wholemeal bagels (or plain or sesame,
  if you prefer)
1 cupful full-fat cream cheese (about
  150g/5½oz)
salt and black pepper

Beat three-quarters of the butter with the mustards, lemon zest, some black pepper and a good seasoning of salt (if you only have salted butter with you, you can leave out the salt).

In a frying pan over a moderate heat, add the remaining butter along with the onion and cook for about 5 minutes, until softened. Add the pieces of salmon to heat through for about 2 minutes, then add the mustard butter and continue cooking for a further 5 minutes or so, until the salmon is hot and the onions are thoroughly soft. Try not to break up the salmon too much more in the pan.

Lightly toast the bagels and spread with the cream cheese, then add the salmon, sprinkle with the lemon juice and sandwich the bagels together to serve.

One-pan fry-up

A good-size, large cast-iron or coated non-stick pan will make serving and sliding out each portion much easier. Cutting the sausages in half lengthways cuts down the cooking time considerably, meaning that, yes, this truly is a one-pan fry-up, serving 2 people, without the endless pots and pans that such a giant breakfast can sometimes require. If you felt like it, you could warm some beans in a pan to go alongside, but this is by no means imperative. Serve with brown sauce or ketchup and good-size chunks of crusty bread and butter to mop.

FEEDS 2

olive, sunflower or vegetable oil,
  for frying
2 sausages, halved lengthways
6 button mushrooms, quartered
  or thickly sliced
4 smoked or unsmoked, streaky
  or back bacon rashers

2 ripe tomatoes, halved and
  seasoned well
2 large free-range eggs
salt and black pepper

TO SERVE
sliced crusty bread, toasted
your favourite condiments

Heat a frying pan over a high heat and get it really hot while you assemble the ingredients.

Add a spot of oil to the pan and place the sausages in the pan, cut-side down. Cook until browned, then flip them over and cook the other side – depending on size, about 2 minutes on each side should do. Tip them out onto a plate.

Add a spot more oil to the pan and add the mushrooms. Cook for about 5 minutes, until the liquid has evaporated and the mushrooms are cooked through. Season with salt and pepper as they cook.

Put the mushrooms to one side with the sausages, wipe out the pan with a bit of kitchen paper (if you have some; not to worry if you don't), then lay the bacon and halved tomatoes, cut-side down, in the pan. Cook for a few minutes, until the bacon is crisp and golden, flipping it over midway through the cooking time. You don't need to flip the tomato – you want just the one side to take on a bit of colour. Return the cooked sausages to the pan and distribute evenly.

Make 2 pockets for the eggs among the ingredients and turn the heat down to moderate–low. Crack an egg into each pocket. Season the eggs with a pinch of salt and a good grind of black pepper and cook to your liking – anywhere from 2–5 minutes. Remove from the heat, slide each portion onto a plate, and serve with sliced crusty bread and butter and your favourite condiments.

Sweet cinnamon eggy bread

Eggy bread is camping gold and a super way to use up slightly stale bread towards the end of the trip. This is the moreish breakfast that many will recognize as a savoury one, served with ketchup, brown or hot sauce. Here, though, I'm giving the sweet version, and I think you and those in your camping party will find it equally delicious.

1 tsp ground cinnamon
1 tbsp plain flour
big pinch of salt
1 tbsp caster (superfine) sugar, plus
  more to sprinkle
4 eggs, lightly beaten

about 3 tbsp whole milk
finely grated zest of ½ lemon
4 thick (about 3cm/1¼in) slices of
  slightly stale white bread
4 tbsp butter

Mix ½ teaspoon of the cinnamon with the flour, salt and sugar. Combine the eggs and milk in a separate bowl and beat in the cinnamon and flour mixture and the lemon zest to form a smooth batter.

Dip the slices of bread into the egg mixture and leave to soak until saturated and soft.

Heat a large frying pan over a moderate heat and add some of the butter. Allow to melt. Working in batches, cook the eggy bread in the pan for about 2 minutes on each side, until soft and golden. Repeat the process with a little more butter and more eggy bread.

Eat hot from the pan, each slice sprinkled with the remaining cinnamon and a little more sugar.

Mushrooms with eggs, feta cheese and chilli butter

This is my favourite breakfast or brunch in the book. Chilli butter is delicious stuff, and the soft, fried mushrooms, feta and runny eggs are exactly the sort of dish it was made for. I like to use field or portobello mushrooms, preferring their dark feathery gills when fried, turning all slippery and full of the fat and chilli flakes, but use button if you prefer.

SERVES 2

4 tbsp butter or olive oil
1 tsp chilli flakes, plus more to sprinkle
4 large or 8 medium mushrooms, thickly sliced
1 bunch of spring onions (scallions), white and green parts separated, all thinly sliced

1 x 200g (7oz) packet of feta, crumbled
big pinch of salt
4 eggs
black pepper
flat breads or pita breads, toasted, to serve

Melt the butter in a frying pan over a moderate heat. Add the chilli flakes and fry for 1 minute until fragrant, then pour off half the melted chilli butter and keep warm.

Add the mushrooms and the white of the spring onions (scallions) to the chilli butter in the pan and cook for 3–5 minutes, until tender and the liquid from the mushrooms has evaporated. Stir in half the feta cheese and the salt and season with black pepper.

Reduce the heat to medium and shake the pan to spread the mushroom mixture in single layer.

Make a little pocket or dent for each egg in the mushroom mixture and break one egg into each. Cook for 3–5 minutes, until the eggs are just about set or cooked to your liking.

Serve topped with the reserved melted chilli butter and the remaining feta and the spring onion greens, and with toasted flat breads or pita breads on the side.

137

Smoked cheese and spring onion eggy bread

With a streak of chilli sauce, this eggy bread is hands down the best savoury version you will ever eat. Scamorza is a southern Italian cow's milk cheese and the smoked version, *scamorza affumicata*, is utterly delicious. It melts as it cooks, behaving in much the same way as mozzarella, but with a subtle smoky background flavour. It's pretty easy to find in the supermarket these days, but if you can't track any down, do use an alternative smoked cheese. With the eggs and bacon, the fried bread is, quite simply, unbeatable.

4 tbsp butter or olive, sunflower or vegetable oil

4 rashers of unsmoked or smoked streaky bacon, finely chopped

1 pack (about 200g/7oz) smoked scamorza, or any other smoked cheese, grated or finely diced

1 garlic clove, very finely chopped

½ bunch spring onions (scallions), trimmed and finely sliced

4 eggs, lightly beaten

splash of whole milk

big pinch of salt, or more to taste

big pinch of black pepper, or more to taste

1 tbsp plain flour

1 tsp sweet or hot, smoked paprika

4 thick (about 3cm/1¼in) slices of slightly stale white bread

Melt half the butter (or heat the oil) in a frying pan over a moderate heat. Add the bacon and fry for about 5 minutes until golden and crisp. Set aside, leaving the fat in the pan.

Mix the cheese, garlic and spring onions (scallions) together in a bowl with the eggs and milk, then mix in the dry ingredients to form a smooth batter. Add the cooked bacon and mix well to combine.

Dip the slices of bread in the bacon and egg mixture and soak until saturated and soft.

Melt the remaining butter in the pan and fry the slices of bread over a moderate heat for about 2 minutes on each side, until golden and crisp (work in batches if you like). Remove from the heat and serve immediately.

5

LUNCHES AND PICNICS

You don't have to leave the campsite to eat any of these dishes, but I did want to write a section that would work well to pack up and take as a picnic on day trips or footloose adventures. So, hearty salads and chunky sandwiches – dishes that you can assemble campside to enjoy later on that day, recipes that can handle a tight squash in a backpack, or are happier for sitting, allowing for flavours to meld and appetites to grow. Cook the eggs, potatoes, pasta, noodles, fried ham and so on that morning, then pack it up in tubs. Come lunchtime, what follows is a casual assembly of ingredients all from a camping-friendly storecupboard of tins, jars and packets, along with some good bread and pretty basic salad ingredients. This is laid-back food – easy, but nonetheless delicious.

Rice noodles with smoked tofu and peanuts

Rice noodles are a wonderful ingredient to take with you camping. Just rehydrate them in some boiled water in a bowl to soften – they really do require minimal effort and equipment. With the noodles soaking, you can then assemble the remaining ingredients before leaving everything to wallow in the liquid for as long as you like. The salad ingredients are suggestions, but do add tofu (I like the smoked version). Leftover barbecued meat would also be good here – use as many or as few of these suggestions as you can feasibly source. Peanuts offer a good salty crunch, although cashews would be equally good.

200g (7oz) vermicelli dried rice noodles (about 4 nests)

about 1 tbsp sesame, sunflower or vegetable oil

200g (7oz) marinated or smoked tofu, diced small (about 1 pack), or leftover roast or grilled meat

any combination of at least 3 of the following:
· a handful of bean sprouts
· a handful of mangetout (snow peas), thinly sliced
· 1 cucumber, peeled, deseeded and thinly sliced
· 1 large carrot, coarsely grated
· 1 small green lettuce, shredded
· ½ bunch of spring onions (scallions), trimmed and thinly sliced
· 5 radishes, thinly sliced or grated
· large handful of edamame, podded (defrosted, if needed)
· handful of roasted salted peanuts or cashews, chopped roughly (optional)

FOR THE DRESSING
juice of 2 limes
1 garlic clove, peeled and crushed to a paste with a little salt
3 tbsp fish sauce
2 tbsp light brown soft sugar
pinch of crushed chilli flakes or chilli sauce, to taste (optional)

Cook the noodles as per the packet instructions, then drain them and refresh them under cold running water. Dress the drained and refreshed noodles with the oil so that they don't stick, then set to one side.

Make the dressing by combining all the ingredients with 4 tablespoons of water and set aside.

Add the tofu and your selection of vegetables to the noodles, mixing in the dressing and stirring well to combine. Add the peanuts or cashews to serve.

Spanish tortilla sandwiches with aioli

Buy good-quality, chunky-cut, salted crisps for this recipe – I like the ones that have been fried with the potato skin still on. I have made many, many tortillas over the years and mostly with potatoes that have been fried in the onion-y oil until very soft, then mixed through with eggs, salt and pepper before being fried in a pan like a thick omelette. I am here to tell you that making a Spanish tortilla with a large packet of crisps is life-changing, especially if you're as keen on making tortillas as I am. The crisps soften and bend obligingly in the egg and onion mixture. They also season the tortilla mixture beautifully, so do remember this when adding extra salt, and go big on the black pepper. Cheat's aioli here, using shop-bought mayonnaise. This is the sandwich to end all sandwiches.

4 tbsp olive oil, plus more to cook
2 large onions, finely sliced, plus more
   if needed
6 eggs, beaten
2 large packets (about 300g/10½oz) of
   thick-cut salted crisps
salt and black pepper

1 good-size baguette, split down the
   middle and cut into 4, to serve

FOR THE AIOLI
5 tbsp mayonnaise
1 large garlic clove, crushed to a paste
   with a little salt

Heat the oil in a good-size (about 22cm/8½in), non-stick frying pan over a moderate–low heat. Add the onion and fry for 12–15 minutes, until very, very soft and just starting to take on a bit of colour. Remove the onions from the heat and put in a large bowl, keeping the oil back in the pan.

Add the eggs to the bowl with the cooked onions and add all of the crisps. Stir to combine, adding plenty of salt and black pepper, but remembering the crisps are salted.

Put the pan with the oil back on the heat, adding a splash more oil if you need – you want the base of the pan to have a 1cm (½in) film. Turn the heat up to high and get the pan very, very hot.

Add the eggs, onion and crisp mixture to the pan, scooping and stirring the mixture with a wooden spoon as it cooks. Do this for about 3 minutes, until about half of the mixture is cooked through, then shuffle the pan to distribute the loose mixture evenly and continue to cook for about 2 minutes, for the base to settle and form a golden crust.

CONTINUED...

Use a plate to fit over the pan and carefully invert the pan upside-down with the tortilla now on the plate. Wipe out the pan with a bit of kitchen paper (if you have some; if not, not to worry) and place it back over a high heat. Add a splash more oil, if necessary – just a couple of tablespoons should do.

Carefully slide the uncooked side of the tortilla back into the pan and shuffle the pan to distribute, tucking the edges neatly into the sides of the pan. Cook the tortilla for another 3–5 minutes, until the underside is golden and the egg is cooked through. It's good to leave the centre still a little soft to the touch, as the egg will continue to cook once removed from the heat.

Invert the cooked tortilla onto a clean plate, then allow to cool a little before cutting into wedges.

Make the aioli. Mix the mayonnaise with the garlic, then tuck wedges of the tortilla into the baguette and slather with the aioli to serve.

Roasted pepper, black olive and Serrano ham squashed sandwich

Wrapping the sandwich tight shut to soak and wallow, just enough, with the rest of the ingredients makes this an outstanding offering. This is a picnic game-changer – the longer you leave it, the better it gets. The ham is optional; do away with it if you like, or add anchovies instead, or marinated artichokes – it's up to you. This is less of a recipe and more of an instruction for making squashed (and the right side of soggy) sandwiches, or *muffuletta* as they are known in Italian.

1 small red onion, very thinly sliced
4 large red (bell) peppers from a jar, drained and roughly sliced
6 tbsp tapenade from a jar, or use roughly chopped pitted black olives
2 tbsp red or white wine vinegar
focaccia or large crusty baguette (to feed 4), split open to fill, but not sliced fully in two

4 large ripe tomatoes, thinly sliced
1 little gem lettuce, finely sliced
250g (9oz) mozzarella ball, drained and cut into 4 thick slices
150g (5½oz; about 12 slices) Serrano or Parma ham (optional)
2–3 tbsp olive oil
salt and black pepper

Mix the onion with the (bell) peppers, tapenade and vinegar, then season with salt and pepper.

Open out the focaccia or baguette. Spread the pepper and onion mixture over the bottom then top with the tomatoes, gem, cheese and ham (if using). Drizzle with oil, then sandwich tight shut, squashing down firmly to enclose. Slice into 4 sandwiches.

Wrap the sandwiches tightly in foil and let rest for at least 1 hour before serving – you want the juices to run into the bread, trust me.

Pasta with peppers, anchovies, olives and capers

Key to a good pasta salad is plenty of plump, tasty ingredients to accompany the cooked pasta, which must be cooked al dente (that is to say, just firm to the bite), because it can then sit in the juices drawing more liquid as it waits to be eaten. A failsafe combination here of slippery-soft, cooked-down peppers, capers, olives and tomatoes is evocative, I like to think, of southern Italy and blazing sunshine.

300g (10½oz) short pasta such as farfalle, orecchiette, rigatoni or penne
3 tbsp olive oil, plus more to serve
2 red, yellow or orange (bell) peppers, deseeded and cut into 1cm (½in) slices
3 large garlic cloves, very thinly sliced
½ tsp dried oregano
15 cherry tomatoes, halved
2 tbsp red wine vinegar

8–12 anchovy fillets, torn in half lengthways
2 tbsp capers
20 pitted black olives (kalamata are nice)
about 100g (3½oz) rocket (arugula) leaves (1 large bag; optional)
salt and black pepper

Cook the pasta according to the packet instructions, keeping to the leaner side of cooking times, then drain and cool as quickly and in as even a layer as possible.

Heat the olive oil in a pan over a moderate–low heat, add the (bell) peppers along with the garlic, oregano and cherry tomatoes and cook for about 15 minutes, until the peppers and tomatoes are very soft. Season well with salt and pepper, then stir in the vinegar and anchovies. Leave to cool to room temperature.

Stir the cooked pepper mixture through the cooked and cooled pasta, being sure to scrape in all the pan juices and mixing well to combine. Add the capers, olives and rocket (arugula; if using) and mix well. Check the seasoning and you're good to go!

Harissa courgette salad with peaches, toasted couscous, and feta cheese

Harissa is marvellous stuff. Hot, with a pungent, sweet heat, it is a paste of red (bell) peppers and chillies with assorted spices that brings huge flavour to everything it touches. There are very many good brands on the market these days, although you could also make your own (there are plenty of recipes, too). Fry the courgettes (zucchini) until they have a bit of colour but retain slight bite. Fry the lemon halves at the same time to make them extra-juicy. This is a gorgeous and substantial salad dish.

5 tbsp olive oil, plus more to drizzle

4 small firm, green or yellow courgettes (zucchini), trimmed and sliced in 1cm (1/2in) slices

finely grated zest of 1 lemon, then cut in half

3 tbsp harissa

1 cupful couscous (about 190g/6½oz)

3 cupfuls water (about 700ml/24fl oz), freshly boiled

3 ripe peaches, stoned and sliced

1 x 200g (7oz) packet feta, crumbled

salt and black pepper

Heat 2 tablespoons of the olive oil in a pan over a moderate–high heat. Add the courgettes (zucchini) and the lemon zest and lemon halves and fry with a generous pinch of salt for about 5 minutes, until the vegetables are lightly browned and soft, but still with some crunch, and the lemon flesh is soft and juicy.

Remove the pan from the heat and set aside the lemons, then add the harissa and remaining olive oil to the pan. Check the seasoning, adding more salt and pepper to taste. Squeeze over the juice from the fried lemons. Transfer the courgettes to a bowl.

Wipe out the pan with kitchen paper or a clean cloth and add the couscous. Toast, stirring, over a medium heat for 3–5 minutes, then add the boiling water to the pan. Remove from the heat, cover, and leave to stand 5 minutes before fluffing with a fork.

To serve or pack up and take with you, mix the cooked courgettes along with all their juices into the couscous, drizzle with oil and top with the peach slices and crumbled feta.

Frankfurter, piccalilli and potato salad

Ahh, this one's a winner. Frankfurters have a great shelf life – real longevity for a meat product, as long as you keep them cool. I'm suggesting you cook the lot – potatoes, eggs and frankfurters – in the same pan (camping, remember?). Just be sure not to crack the eggs as you place them in the pan (a very messy outcome). Don't worry about cooking the other two ingredients with the whole eggs – you are boiling the contents of the pan, killing off any possible bacteria.

600g (1lb 5oz) waxy small new
  potatoes
4 eggs
6 frankfurters
1 bunch of spring onions (scallions),
  trimmed and thinly sliced
3 tbsp olive oil
2 tbsp red wine vinegar
salt and black pepper

TO SERVE
4 tbsp piccalilli
4–6 tbsp sour cream

Bring a large pan of well-salted water to the boil. Add the potatoes and the eggs. After 8–9 minutes, remove the eggs from the water, then refresh in cold water, drain, cool and peel. Continue cooking the potatoes for a further 7–11 minutes, until tender. For the final 3 minutes of the potato cooking time, add the frankfurters to the pan, letting them warm through.

Drain the potatoes and slice the frankfurters into good-size lengths of about 2–3cm (3/4–1 1/4in) and chop the potatoes into bite-size pieces.

Tip the mixture into a bowl and mix through the spring onions (scallions), seasoning to taste with salt and plenty of pepper. Add the olive oil and vinegar, mixing well to combine. Halve the boiled eggs.

Serve the frankfurter mixture in bowls with a couple of tablespoons of piccalilli and a big blob of sour cream, along with the halved boiled eggs on the side.

Devilled egg with tinned crab, Dijon and potatoes

I'm loathe to use the word deconstructed in any recipe, but it is a helpful analogy here if you take it to mean making a dish that is easier and quicker to assemble – perhaps outdoors, on a picnic table – than its constructed cousin. Good-quality tinned crab is a boon for the camping storecupboard, especially in locations where fresh, locally caught fish is not so readily available (although if it is – choose fresh and local every time).

400g (14oz) waxy small new potatoes
6 eggs
2 x 145g (5oz) cans of crab (or tuna,
  mackerel or anchovies), drained
6 tbsp crème fraîche or mayonnaise
4 tsp Dijon mustard
½ bunch of spring onions (scallions),
  trimmed and thinly sliced
salt and black pepper
sweet or hot, smoked or unsmoked
  paprika, to serve

Bring a large pan of well-salted water to the boil. Add the potatoes and the eggs. After 8–9 minutes, remove the eggs from the water, refresh in cold water, drain, cool and peel. Continue cooking the potatoes for a further 7–11 minutes until tender. Drain, leave to cool, then when cool enough to handle, cut in half.

Cut the eggs in half lengthways and place them in a serving bowl along with the potatoes, then top with the crab meat.

Divide the salad into portions and add a good-size spoonful of mayonnaise to each. Top generously with Dijon, then season with salt and pepper. Sprinkle with the sliced spring onions (scallions) and serve liberally dusted with paprika.

Salami, artichoke and mascarpone bagels

Winningly simple assembly in this recipe. Be sure to season the mascarpone with plenty of black pepper, and do use some of the oil in the jar of artichokes to drizzle over the sandwich ingredients before closing tightly shut. You can use jarred, pickled or antipasti mushrooms in place of the salami, if you prefer. Wrapped, these bagels will be extremely good for a few hours or more. You can, if you like, also wrap them in foil, and chuck them in the embers of the fire or on a grill to soften just a little. Up to you.

4 wholemeal bagels, sliced in half
1 tub (250g/9oz) mascarpone or full-fat
  cream cheese
16 slices of salami
8 grilled artichokes in oil (roughly
  1 jar), drained (oil reserved) and
  roughly chopped
salt and black pepper

Spread the bottom halves of the bagels with the mascarpone and season well with salt and plenty of pepper.

Add the salami and the artichokes, then drizzle each bagel with a little of the artichoke oil and sandwich shut to serve (or wrap to travel).

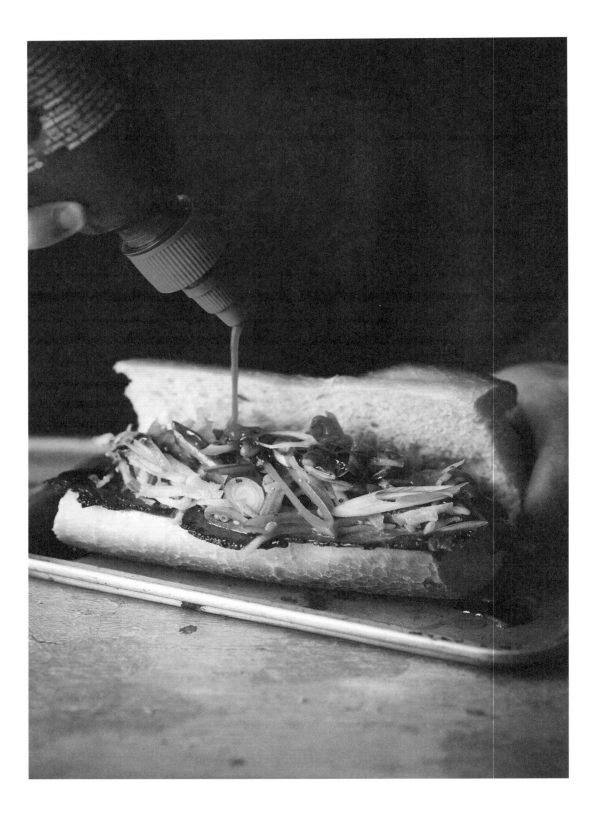

Fried ham with pickled vegetables and hoisin in a baguette

This sandwich goes by the name of *bahn mi* in Vietnam, which can refer to the bread, but also a version of a sub roll stuffed with various savoury ingredients – cooked pork or ham, say; sometimes pâté; and also pickled vegetables with hoisin and hot sauce. Do try to get hold of some thick-cut ham, as this will give the sandwich enough heft – thin, straggly-cut ham just won't do it. I like quite a bit of hot sauce on mine, sriracha to be precise.

1 bunch of spring onions (scallions), trimmed and thinly sliced
1 cucumber, peeled, deseeded and coarsely grated
1 large carrot, peeled and coarsely grated
juice of 1 lime
2 tbsp fish sauce
1 tbsp light brown soft sugar or runny honey
plenty of black pepper or chilli flakes

1 large baguette (to feed 4), sliced to sandwich
5 tbsp hoisin sauce, or use light or dark soy sauce mixed 50:50 with runny honey
8 slices of thick-cut ham (about 250g/9oz)
vegetable oil, for frying
3 tbsp sriracha or another chilli sauce, or more to taste

Mix the spring onions (scallions), cucumber and carrot with the lime juice, fish sauce and sugar and 2 tablespoons of water. Season with black pepper or chilli flakes to taste.

Spread the cut sides of the baguette with half the hoisin sauce. Pour the remaining hoisin sauce into a bowl and toss in the ham to coat.

Heat a splash of oil in a frying pan over a moderate–high heat. Add the ham and fry for 2–3 minutes, until golden brown, even a little crisp on the outside. Remove from the heat and place evenly along the length of the baguette. Add the salad ingredients, again evenly along the length, then add plenty of chilli sauce to taste. Sandwich the baguette shut and cut it into 4 equal pieces to serve.

Tuna, jarred peppers, chickpeas and pickled lemon with gem lettuce

This is a wonderful combination, and good-quality tuna from a sustainable source is a saving grace for any keen camper. There is a way with tuna, tinned or jarred, that doesn't just involve mayonnaise and cucumber, and this is it. The (bell) peppers, chickpeas (garbanzos) and pickled lemon all, like the tuna, come from the storecupboard. As for the lettuce, gem lettuces are pretty bombproof. With small, ribbed leaves, tightly compacted, these little lettuces stay in shape and can handle a bit of a squash when packing up to go – so again, a good camping ingredient.

1 small red onion, very thinly sliced
2 x 400g (14oz) cans of chickpeas (garbanzos), drained and rinsed
2 garlic cloves, very thinly sliced
20 cherry tomatoes, halved
2 tbsp finely chopped preserved lemon
1 small jar or can of roasted red (bell) peppers, drained and sliced (piquillo peppers are excellent)

juice and finely grated zest of 1 lemon
3 small cans (about 350g/12oz altogether) sustainable tuna in oil
1 gem lettuce, shredded
about 3 tbsp olive oil, or use the oil in the tuna tin
salt and black pepper

Place the red onion in a small bowl and cover with cold water. Sprinkle liberally with salt to soften the flavour while you prepare the salad.

In a large mixing bowl combine the chickpeas (garbanzos), garlic, tomatoes, preserved lemon and (bell) peppers and the juice and zest of the lemon, and season to taste with salt and pepper.

Drain the onion and add it to the chickpeas in the bowl.

Drain the tuna and flake the fish into the bowl. Add the lettuce and the olive oil or the oil from the tuna and mix well to serve.

Smoked mackerel pâté with horseradish and cucumber in brown rolls

My three children really love smoked mackerel, and smoked mackerel pâté to be exact. Smoked fish is a terrific camping ingredient because – you guessed it – it has a longer shelf life than fresh. This is a gorgeous sandwich filling, and soft brown rolls and sliced cucumber are as fine a match as any.

4 tbsp butter
1 garlic clove, finely sliced
pinch chilli flakes, or use sweet
   unsmoked paprika
2 tbsp horseradish sauce
300g (10½oz) smoked mackerel fillets,
   skin removed and deboned

6 tbsp crème fraîche or sour cream
juice and finely grated zest of 1 lemon
salt and black pepper
4 soft brown rolls, split open, to serve
½ cucumber, thinly sliced, to serve

Melt the butter in a small pan over a low heat. Add the garlic and chilli flakes or paprika and cook for 3–5 minutes, until the garlic has softened. Remove from the heat, stir in the horseradish and leave to stand for the flavours to infuse, but without letting it cool and set.

Flake the mackerel into a bowl, give it a rough mash with a fork if necessary and add the crème fraîche or sour cream and the lemon juice and zest. Season well with salt and plenty of pepper. Finally, vigorously beat in the flavoured butter, mixing well to combine.

Put the pâté to one side for at least 20–30 minutes for the flavours to meld and the pâté to firm up as the butter cools.

To serve, smear pâté into each roll, topping the pâté with slices of cucumber before sandwiching shut.

PICTURED ON PAGE 169

Bloody Mary prawn and lettuce sub rolls

Take a bag of frozen cooked jumbo prawns (shrimp) with you camping to defrost, then use them for this recipe and you will look like you have your priorities right. The Bloody Mary dressing is a bold and fiery match for the sweet and juicy prawns. Always (always) buy fish from a sustainable source – this is a sandwich you can be proud of, camping or otherwise.

FOR THE DRESSING
3 tbsp sherry or red wine vinegar
1–2 tbsp horseradish sauce, or more to taste
1 tsp Worcestershire sauce
1 tsp Tabasco or other hot-pepper sauce, or to taste
1 tsp Dijon mustard
3 tbsp mayonnaise

FOR THE FILLING
400g (14oz) ready-to-eat cooked prawns (shrimp)

3 ripe tomatoes, diced small
1 cucumber, peeled, deseeded and diced small
½–1 small red onion, finely sliced
handful of pitted green olives, roughly chopped
salt and black pepper

TO SERVE
½ iceberg or 1 large gem lettuce, leaves separated
1 large baguette, split open and cut into 4, or 4 small rolls

Mix together all the ingredients for the dressing in a bowl, then add the filling ingredients and season generously with pepper and perhaps some more salt, remembering that the olives will add seasoning.

Add a few leaves of lettuce to each sandwich or roll and pile the filling on top, along with plenty of the dressing. Sandwich shut and serve.

6

SWEETS AND TREATS

What's wrong with a packet of biscuits, big bar of chocolate and a bag of marshmallows? We're camping, let's keep things easy, some might say. Some, but not many, I expect, if you've bought or borrowed this cookbook.

Camping is exactly the time when you want to knock up a good sweet treat for everyone to share; or take the time to make such an exceptional hot chocolate that it will be remembered many months later on a cold, dank day in November, when a fond memory or a child asking you boundless questions might prompt "do you remember when you made those... round the campfire that night with... when we were camping in...". Recipes – and the moments when we shared that particular food or dish – often accompany the best sorts of memories. That's certainly true in our family, and I'm sure in many others, too.

The recipes in this chapter all rely heavily on the camper van storecupboard, making them very easy, requiring just a modicum of titivating. Nonetheless, they will deliver a dessert or drink that wouldn't look out of place served at home in more routine splendour. In this chapter, certainly more so than the previous, the recipes are usually about assembling some of our favourite dessert ingredients in a no-nonsense fashion and doing this with as little equipment as possible. At the very least, I don't think there is a dish here that won't prompt a great big grin and receptive hands from any of your fellow campers who are fond of a sweet treat.

My favourites are the No-cook Lemon Custard Cheesecake (page 193) and the Raspberry Ripple Evaporated Milk Rice Pudding (page 196). As for the Stroopwaffles with Fried Banana and Dulce de Leche (page 188) – ludicrously easy, and off-the-scale delicious. None of these recipes is shy on the sugar – a treat, as suggested in the title of this chapter – so don't forget your toothbrushes. After all, who doesn't love brushing their teeth in the dark while wearing a head torch?

Hot chocolate with Nutella, hazelnuts and chocolate buttons

This counts as a dessert just as much as it does a hot chocolate – made extra-silky and luscious with a large dollop of Nutella, before being given the squirty-cream treatment, an aerosol of frothy delight that seems to be universally popular with children (some adults, too), and a pretty useful camping ingredient, being UHT. Did I mention the hazelnuts and chocolate buttons on the top? If you asked my kids which is the most memorable moment from shooting this camping book, it might well be this – in the forest with the fire burning and the owls just beginning to hoot.

MAKES 4 BIG CUPS

4 cupfuls whole milk, or use oat,
  hazelnut or UHT (about 1 litre/
  35fl oz)
4 tbsp drinking chocolate
4 tsp Nutella
1 can of aerosol whipped cream
handful of hazelnuts, toasted, skinned
  and roughly chopped (about
  40g/1½oz)
small handful dark (bittersweet) or milk
  chocolate buttons (about 30g/1oz)

Warm the milk with the drinking chocolate in a small pan over a moderate heat, mixing well to combine until very hot.

Pour the hot chocolate into 4 mugs and add a teaspoonful of Nutella to each. Top with a silly amount of whipped cream and sprinkle with the nuts and the chocolate buttons. You will need a spoon!

Mulled apple juice with maple syrup

Simple but always popular, steaming mugs of spiced apple juice are welcome any time of the day – but more so when the sun begins to set and there is a chill in the air. Studding the apples with the cloves gives a gentle spice as the juice heats up – they are decorative and will keep the cloves in place when you come to pour out. A stick of cinnamon, a bay leaf and a vanilla pod – any or all of these will also work. A slug of maple syrup is especially good, too, and any adults might like to add a slosh of rum, whisky or brandy.

MAKES 4 BIG CUPS

2 small apples
4 whole cloves
1 litre (35fl oz) apple juice (I like cloudy)
1 cinnamon stick or good-size pinch of
   ground cinnamon
1 bay leaf
1 vanilla pod (optional)
4 tbsp, or a very generous slug of maple
   syrup or runny honey

Stud the apples with the cloves and put these in a pan along with all of the remaining ingredients. Warm over a moderate heat for about 5 minutes, until piping hot, then serve.

Peppermint teabag hot chocolate

My daughter Ivy is the world's number-one fan of mint-flavoured chocolate anything, and ice cream is her absolute favourite. Ice cream is a little difficult to pull off when it comes to camping, which is why we came up with this hot chocolate recipe instead – pretty much now a camping staple. I say recipe, but really, it could not be any simpler. Make good hot chocolate and steep mint tea bags in the pan while you do so. Use 1 mint tea bag per person, for the flavour to permeate and expel a good shiver of mint to each serving.

MAKES 4 BIG CUPS

4 cupfuls whole milk, or use oat or
   UHT (about 1 litre/35fl oz)
4 tbsp drinking chocolate
4 peppermint tea bags (rip off the tags)

Warm the milk with the drinking chocolate and the mint tea bags in a small pan over a moderate heat, mixing well to combine until very hot. Remove the tea bags and pour the minty hot chocolate into the mugs to serve.

Hot cross buns with melted marshmallow

Hot cross buns do mostly seem to be available year-round in the shops these days. That said, if you can't find them, any soft fruit bun or spiced saffron bun (thinking of Cornwall here)... goodness, any soft bun, with or without fruit – will work, because, to be honest, it's the marshmallows that are the real draw.

16 regular-sized marshmallows
4 hot cross buns or similar, sliced
  in half

Place 4 marshmallows in each bun. Wrap each bun in foil and warm through in the embers of the fire or on a medium–hot grill for about 5 minutes, until the marshmallows are melted and very, very gooey. Remove from the heat and eat – with napkins!

Stroopwaffles with fried banana and dulce de leche

Stroopwaffles are Dutch waffled caramel biscuits – two thin waffles sandwiched together with caramel. Dulce de leche is wicked stuff – cooked and lightly caramelized condensed milk, it is an instant dessert on a spoon. Frying the banana in a bit of salted butter and sprinkle of brown sugar, then loading the caramelized slices each onto a stroopwaffle with a dollop of dulce de leche... well, you'll definitely need a surf, or a long walk, jog or run, just to be on the safe side, won't you?

good-size knob of butter (ideally salted)
1 or 2 stroopwaffles per person
½ banana per person, sliced lengthways
big pinch of soft light brown sugar
1 heaped tsp dulce de leche per
   stroopwaffle

Melt the butter in a frying pan over a moderate heat. Add the banana slices cut-side down and the sugar and cook for about 1½ minutes, until the undersides of the bananas are soft and slightly caramelized. Carefully turn over the slices and cook on the other side for another 1½ minutes, then remove from the heat.

To serve, add the caramelized banana to each stroopwaffle along with with a dollop of dulce de leche.

Malt loaf toasted and stuffed with chocolate buttons

I love this recipe. It's not *really* a recipe, more an assembly of ingredients and – be warned – it can be very messy to serve and to eat. The sprinkled demerara gives the squidgy loaf some extra crunch when it is unwrapped from the foil. Molten and wickedly delicious.

4 tbsp butter, softened
3 tbsp demerara sugar
2 x 260g (9¼oz) loaves of malt loaf,
  thickly sliced
about 120g (4¼oz) dark (bittersweet)
  or milk chocolate buttons (1 large
  packet)

Grease two large sheets of foil with a little of the butter. Use the remainder to butter alternate sides of the malt loaf. Sprinkle each slice with a good pinch of sugar, then make sandwiches using the chocolate buttons. Regroup the slices back into a loaf and wrap each loaf in the buttered foil.

Place the wrapped parcels in the embers of the fire or over a medium–hot grill and cook for 6–8 minutes, turning every couple of minutes, until the chocolate is melted and the malt loaf is hot through, even slightly toasted in parts. Remove from the heat, unwrap and serve.

No-cook lemon custard cheesecake

Who can say among your camping groupies that they've ever been served freshly made lemon cheesecake campside? I think this might well be a world first. Cooling will help to firm these little cheesecakes, but you're camping, so it's my guess the outside evening temperature will be a little on the chillier side. If you have a cool box or fridge, all the better, but it is by no means essential. A prescriptive set of weights and measures is not helpful here. Instead, think in spoonfuls and per person. For four people, I think 2 biscuits and a tablespoon each of the filling.

8 digestive biscuits (graham
  crackers), crushed
1 tbsp melted butter
4 heaped tbsp full-fat cream cheese
1 tbsp caster (superfine) sugar
small pot of custard (about 125g/4½oz)
4 tbsp lemon curd, plus 4 tsp for
  the top

Put the crushed biscuits in a bowl and add the melted butter, mixing to combine. Divide the mixture equally into 4 small cups or ramekins.

In a bowl, beat together the cream cheese, sugar and custard, then stir through the lemon curd.

Top each portion of biscuits with one quarter of the cream cheese mixture, spreading it out over the base. Add 1 teaspoon of lemon curd to the top of each, and put to one side in a cool (refrigerated is even better) place for at least 30 minutes to firm up a little before serving.

Cherry chocolate mess

This is a mess, but a good-looking one. Jars of good-quality chocolate sauce are fairly easy to get hold of these days – I used a dark (bittersweet) chocolate and sea salt one. Homemade (or even shop-bought) meringues are smashed up and mixed with the chocolate and cherries, then finished with an ebullient burst of frothy cream. A mess, as I said.

1 x about 200g (7oz) jar of good-quality
  chocolate sauce
12 mini meringues
1 x 440g (15½oz) can of stoneless black
  cherries in light syrup, drained
1 can of aerosol whipped cream

If the chocolate sauce in the jar is a little on the firm side, stand the jar in some warm water to soften until it is a spoonable consistency.

In a bowl, roughly break up the meringues. Add the drained cherries and the chocolate sauce, then finally the squirty cream. Mix briefly to combine. Serve in bowls or cups.

Raspberry ripple evaporated milk rice pudding

Evaporated milk (an ingredient with an old-fashioned reputation) is canned milk that has had 60 per cent of the water content removed. Unlike condensed milk, it hasn't had any sugar added. In rice pudding, made here like a risotto on the stove top, the evaporated milk saturates and cooks the rice to perfection, lending deeply milky, almost toffee notes. As for the raspberry jam – I say a ripple, but my kids will always shout for a river.

generous ½ cup risotto rice (about
    100g/3½oz)
2 x 170g (6oz) cans of evaporated milk
1 tbsp caster (superfine) sugar
raspberry (or any) jam, as much as
    you like

Put the rice and the evaporated milk in a pan over a medium heat. Fill each milk can up with cold water and add the water to the pan, too. Bring the liquid to the boil, then reduce the heat and stir often over a low heat for 18–20 minutes, until the rice is tender and the liquid is almost all absorbed. Add a splash more water to the pan if you think it needs it during the cooking time.

Stir through the sugar and remove from the heat, setting the rice pudding to one side for a few minutes to settle and cool just a little – warm is ideal. To serve, stir through a spoonful (or more) of jam per person.

Index

Suppliers

VW. Dreamy wheels.

TOAST. Warm knits.

Netherton Foundry. Camping cookware and a fearsome *chapa*.

Joy Stoves. A joy to cook on.

Falcon Enamel. The only enamel.

Primus. Very cool, that Onja gas stove.

Campingaz and **Coleman** for iconic lanterns.

Eweleaze Campsite, Dorset. Wide open skies, a terrific campsite.

Belmont Estate, Somerset. We asked for woods, and we got them.

Pipers Farm. Brilliant butcher.

Fish For Thought. Spanking fresh fish.

Isle of Wight Tomatoes. Number 1.

Acknowledgements

Sarah, Jane and Tim, Sam's family, for the secluded beach location. And for letting Dot and Ivy borrow Barney the dog.

The team at **Quadrille**, in particular, Sarah Lavelle and Claire Rochford. If anyone can pull a camping cookbook together in a year when travel plans and holidays were in a constant state of flux, it is you.

Sam Folan. Photographer and now friend. My girls adore you. Rule of six, and what a six we were, such fun camping with you – again soon.

Faye Wears. For prop styling from afar.

Our children: **Grace, Ivy and Dorothy.** We've had stellar sunsets, flooded music festivals, paella on the beach, and also on one occasion "the worst holiday ever". Here's to the three of you, for camping through thick and thin. Always.

Publishing Director Sarah Lavelle
Editor Stacey Cleworth
Copy-editor Judy Barratt
Proofreader Susan Low
Design and Art Direction Claire Rochford
Photographer Sam Folan
Prop Stylist Faye Wears
Head of Production Stephen Lang
Production Controller Katie Jarvis

Published in 2021 by Quadrille, an imprint of Hardie Grant Publishing

Quadrille
52–54 Southwark Street
London SE1 1UN
quadrille.com

Cataloguing in Publication Data: a catalogue record for this book is available from The British Library.

Text © Claire Thomson and Matt Williamson 2021
Photography © Sam Folan 2021
Design © Quadrille 2021

ISBN 978 1 78713 684 7
Printed in China